White Water Pyrénées

A rivers guidebook for kayakers and rafters

by Patrick Santal

Translated by
Norman, Pamela and David Taylor,
White Rose Canoe Club, Leeds, England.

Editor: Peter Knowles
Contributior: Phil Quil

Translated from 'Pyrénées Rivières Sauvages' the original
French guidebook by Patrick Santal, published in 1999 by the
Association Rivières Sauvages ou Kayak Sans Frontières.

Drawings and cartoons are by Alan Fox (Foxy).

Photographs - see opposite.

Maps - see acknowledgements page.

Published simultaneously by Rivers Publishing UK. & Menasha Ridge Press USA.

Catalogued in the British Library. ISBN: 0-9519413-5-6.

Catalogued in the Library of Congress, USA. ISBN: 0-89732-342-4.

Printed by Bell and Bain Ltd, Thornliebank, Scotland.

Trade enquiries:

- **U.K. and Europe**: to Cordee Outdoor Books & Maps,

  3a De Montford St, Leicester LE1 7HD, UK, Fax: 0116 247 1176.

- **North America**: to Menasha Ridge Press,

  700 South 28th Street, Suite 206, Birmingham, AL 35233, USA, Fax: 205 326 1012

- **Other countries**: to Rivers Publishing U.K.

  125 Hook Rise South, Surbiton, Surrey KT6 7NA, UK, Fax: +44 208 391 5114.

Disclaimer

The information and advice given in this book were written in good faith, but the reader is warned that nothing in this book should be regarded as 100% accurate: this book was written by humans so there are bound to be errors, rivers and rapids change, and some information is out of date before it is printed.

All advice and information should be treated with caution and checked locally. The publishers, authors and contributors can accept no responsibility for any loss, injury, or inconvenience sustained by any person as a result of information or advice contained in this guide.

A typographic error in the guidebook had forced Henry into a difficult situation ......

Warning: *Printed using Laser-phobic ink - this may degrade if scanned by photocopiers or similar devices.*

Photographs

Gilles Falkenreck - pages A2 upper, D4 lower, 134.

Andrès Sio Gonzalez - pages A3, A4, B3, D3 upper, D1, 52, 76, 81, 122.

Marie-Pierre Guinchard - pages 86, 157.

Jean Vaxélaire - page B1, and the back cover.

Joce Lorin - page C3 upper.

Evelyne Grard - page 62.

Patrick Santal - All other photographs are by the author.

Note: colour photographs are located:
A1 - A4 between pages 32 and 33.
B1 - B4 between pages 64 and 65.
C1 - C4 between pages 96 and 97.
D1 - D4 between pages 128 and 129.

Acknowledgements

The 'Association 'Rivieres Sauvages or Kayak Sans Frontieres' would like to acknowledge and thank all the kayakers who worked together to produce and create this guide - without their help neither the French edition nor this one would have been possible :

Les Béarnais :

Michel Alzuyet, Philippe Arrhie, Gilles Falkenreck, Luc Gabette, Evelyne Grard, Marie-Pierre Guinchard, Thierry Hanon, Dominique Laffite, Pierre Pola, Jean Preux, Patrick Santal, Andrès Sio-Gonzalez, Hélène Sio-Gonzalez, Jean Vaxelaire

Les Bordelais :

Safia Azizi, Jean Marie Bel, Didier Lagassan, Ulrike Paetsch,

Les Toulousains :

Jean-Paul Giondini (l'Ours), François Giondini (l'Ourson), Dominique Grange, Yves Jenvrin, Gilles Pierrat.

Andrès Sio Gonzalez - for maps of the río Aragón Subordán upper section, río Canal Roya, río Gállego (above Biescas), and río Sia.
François Giondini - for maps of the Neste d'Aure and Neste de Louron.
Antxon - for maps of the río Iraty, río Urrobi, río Esca, and río Estos
Angel Cheliz - for maps of the Barranco de Llert and río Isabeña - section B.
Bertrand Delignière - for maps of the Aude and the Têt.
Gérome Fratty - for information on the Nive.
Dhrari Benyounes - for checking and correcting the bassin du Salat.

Also a big thank you to the many paddlers who were present on the occasion of a river descent but are not named above.

À Jean-Luc,

Et à tous les autres ...

Introduction
Summary of rivers 8
How to use this guide   15
Kayaking in the Pyrenees 17
Planning your trip 19
Notes on Countries 22
North Coast of Spain 25
Flore and fauna 28
Hydrology 29
Rafting 31

FRENCH RIVERS

Bassin de la Nive 33
La Grande Nive 35
Río Urrizate 37
Le Bastan 37
Nive des Aldudes 38
Nive d'Esterençuby 38

Bassin du Saison 39
Gave du Saison 41
Gave de Larrau 42
Gave de Ste. Engrace 43

Bassin du Gave d'Oloron 45
Gave d'Oloron 48
Gave d'Aspe 49
Gave du Lourdios 51
Gave d'Aydius 51
Gave du Brousset 53
Gave d'Ossau 55

Bassin de Pau 57
Gave de Pau 60
l'Ouzom 61
Gave d'Arrens 61
Gave d'Azun 62
Gave de Cauterets 63
Gave du Bastan 65
Gave d'Heas 67
Gave de Gavarnie 68

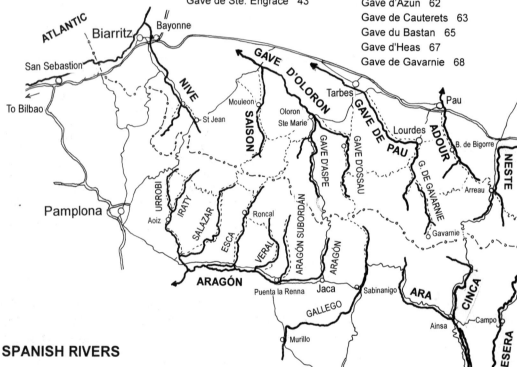

SPANISH RIVERS

Bassin Río Aragon 110
Urrobi 114
Iraty 115
Urtxuria 117
Salazar 118
Esca 119
Veral 120
Aragón Subordán 121
Aragón 123
Canal Roya 123

Bassin Río Gallego 124
Río Gallego 126

Bassin Río Ara 129
Ara 131
Forcos 133

Bassin Río Cinca 135
Cinca 138
Cinqueta 139
Aso 142
Vellos 142
Barrosa 143
Irues 143

Bassin Río Esera 145
Esera 147
Vallibierna 147
Estos 148
Barranco de Viú 148
Barbaruens 149
Barranco de Llert 149
Isabeña 151

**Bassin Río Noguera
Ribagorçana 152**
Baliera 155
Noguera de Tor 156

Bassin de l'Adour 71
l'Adour 73
l'Adour de Lesponne 73

Bassin des Nestes 75
la Neste d'Aure 77
la Neste de Louron 78
Rioumajou 80

Bassin de la Garonne 82
l'Ourse 84
le Ger 84
Río Varrados 85

Bassin du Salat 87
le Riberot 90
le Salat 90
l'Estours 92
l'Arac 93
le Garbet 93
l'Alet 94
le Cors 95

Bassin de l'Ariege 97
l'Ariege 100
l'Oriege 100
le Vicdessos 101
l'Aston 102

Bassin Mediterraneen 103
l'Aude 106
le Rebenty 107
la Tet 108
le Tech 109

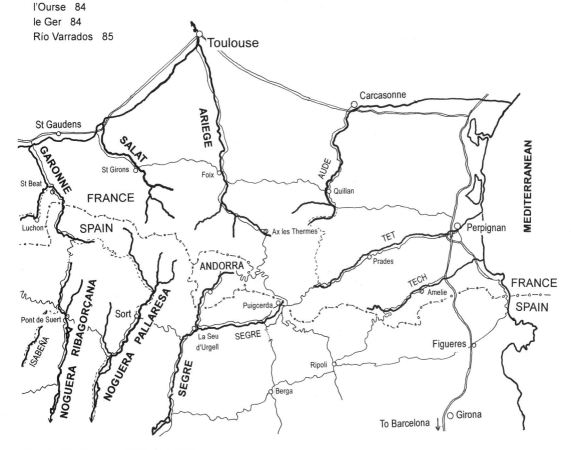

Bassin Río Noguera Pallaresa 157
Noguera Pallaresa 162
Caregue 164
Lladorre 164
Noguera de Vallferrera 165
Noguera de Tor 165
Santa Magdalena 166
Manyanet 166
Bellera 167

Bassin Río Segre 168
Segre 172
Le Carol 173
Lavansa 173
Valira Del Nord 174

Appendices
A Books and Maps 175
B Contributors 176
C Glossary 178

Index 180

French Rivers

River Basin	River	km	Difficulty	WW Stars	Scenery
Nive	Grande Nive A - from St Jean	10	II (3)	*	**
	B - from Osses	7	II - III	**	**
	C - from Bidarray	10	II (3+) D	*	**
	D - from Itxassou	4	II	*	**
	Río Urrizate	3	IV - V	**	***
	Le Bastan	4	III - III+	**	**
	Nive des Aldudes	8	II - III (4) D	*	**
	Nive d'Esterençuby	9	III - IV	*	**
Saison	Gave du Saison	9	III D	**	*
	Gave de Larrau A - Upper	4	IV (x)	**	***
	B - Classic	6	III (4) D	**	**
	Gave de St Engrace A - Upper	2.5	IV (5) E	**	***
	B - Classic	6	IV - V (6)	***	**
Gave d'Oloron	Gave d'Oloron	40	II - III D	**	**
	Gave d'Aspe A - upper	7	IV (5)	**	**
	B - from Fort du Portalet	15	III - IV (5) (x) D	***	***
	C - from Bedous	12	II - III	**	**
	D - from Soeix	4	II - III	**	**
	Gave du Lourdios	8.5	III - IV (4+) D	**	*
	Gave d'Aydius	4	IV - V D	**	*
	Gave du Brousset A - upper	4	IV	***	***
	B - to Gabas	1.5	V (6) (x)	**	**
	Gave d'Ossau A - from Gabas	4	IV - V (x) E	***	***
	B - les Eaux-Chaudes	6.5	IV (5) (x)	***	***
	C - from Laruns	11	II - III D	**	**
	D - from Buzy	18	II - III (4) D	***	***
Gave de Pau	Gave de Pau A - from Pierrefitte	20	II - III D	**	*
	B - from Lourdes	14	II - III D	**	**
	L'Ouzom	7.5	III - IV	**	**
	Gave d'Arrens	4.5	IV - IV+ D	**	**
	Gave d'Azun	5	IV (5) D	**	**
	Gave de Cauterets A - upper	800m	V - VI	***	**
	B - Classic	6	V - V+ D	***	**
	C- middle gorges	2	IV (5) (6) D	**	**
	D - lower gorges	3	IV - V E	***	**
	Gave du Bastan	4	V	***	**
	Gave d'Heas	1.5	V (x) E	**	***
	Gave de Gavarnie A - classic	4	IV (5)	***	***
	B - from Gedre	3.5	IV	***	**
	C - from Pragneres	2	IV - V	***	**
	D - Gorges de Sia	2.5	V (6) (x) E	***	**
	E - Gorges de Luz	7.5	IV - IV+ E D	***	***

French Rivers

River Basin	River	km	Difficulty	WW Stars	Scenery
Adour	l'Adour	11	III - III+ (D)	**	**
	l'Adour de Lesponne	10	IV (5)	***	**
Nestes	Neste d'Aure A - from St Lary	12	II - III D	**	**
	B- from Areau	6	II - III	**	*
	Neste de Louron A - from Pont de Prat	4	V (6) (x)	**	**
	B - from hot springs	3	II+ D	**	**
	C - from Lac de Loudenvielle	5	II (3) D	**	**
	D - from Avajan	8	II - III (4)	**	**
	Rioumajou	7	IV - V (x) E D	*	**
Garonne	l'Ourse	9	II - III D	*	*
	le Ger	9	IV - V E D	***	**
	Río Varrados	3.5	IV (5)	**	**
Salat	le Riberot	5	IV - V (5+)	***	**
	le Salat A - upper	3	V (6) D	***	**
	B - from Salau	4.5	IV D	**	**
	C - from Couflens	5.5	III - IV	**	**
	D - from Pont de la Taule	11	II - III D	*	**
	l'Estours A - upper	1.5	IV+ (5)	***	***
	B - from the dam	4	IV - V	**	**
	l'Arac	12	II - III D	**	**
	le Garbet A - from Aulus les Bains	8	III -IV (5) E D	**	**
	B - from Erce	7	III (4)	**	**
	l'Alet A - from Stillom	2.5	III (5)	**	**
	B - from Serac d'Ustou	8	II - III - IV	***	**
	le Cors (or Haut Alet)	4	IV - V (6)	**	**
Ariege	l'Ariege	8.5	IV - V (D)	**	**
	l'Oriege	6	III - IV	**	**
	le Vicdessos A - from Montcalm	6	IV - V (6)	**	**
	B - from Auzat	15	II - III - IV (6) D	*	*
	l'Aston	5	IV - V (x)	**	**
Mediterraneen	l'Aude A - upper	9	III+	**	*
	B -from Gesse	4	III	**	*
	C -from Nantilla	6	II - III D	**	*
	D - Defile de Pierre Lys	6	II - III - IV	**	**
	le Rebenty	7	II - III (4)	*	*
	la Tet	2	III (4) (5+)	**	**
	le Tech	6	III-IV-V (5+) D E	**	**

*** = Outstanding

** = Recommended

* = Limited interest

Spanish Rivers

River Basin	River	km	Difficulty	WW stars	Scenery
Río Aragon	Urrobi A - upper	6	III - IV	**	**
	B - from Arrieta	7	II - III D	*	*
	C - from d'Arce	7.5	III - IV (x)	*	*
	Iraty A - upper	11	III - IV (5)	*	***
	B - from Irabia dam	14	III D	**	**
	C - from Arive	14	III - IV D	**	*
	D - from d'Usoz dam	7	III	**	*
	E - from d'Aoiz	22	II	**	*
	F - from Lumbier	12	II - II E D	**	**
	Urtxuria	6	III - IV (x) E	***	***
	Salazar A - from Biguesa bridge	8	III+ (4+) E D	**	***
	B - from Usun bridge	8	II	*	*
	Esca A - from Isaba	18	III - IV D	**	**
	- from Burgui	7	III - IV D	**	**
	C - from Salvatierra	3.5	IV	**	**
	Veral A - upper	12	IV - V	***	***
	B - from first road bridge	12	III (4+) E	**	**
	C - lower	5	II - III	**	***
	Aragón Subordán A - upper	3	III (4)	**	***
	B - Red gorge	5	IV (5) (x) E	**	**
	C - from Boca	25	II - III (4)	**	**
	Aragón	17	II+	*	**
	Canal Roya	2	IV - IV+ (6)	**	**
Rio Gallego	Gallego A - from Sta Helena	5	III+	*	*
	B - Classic	7	II - III (4)	**	***
	C - lower	5	II (3)	*	*
Río Ara	Ara A - upper	4	IV - V (5+) (x) E	***	***
	B - 'the Slabs'	3	IV - V (6) (x)	***	***
	C - from Los Navarros bridge	7	IV (5) D	***	**
	D - from Broto	15	II - III - IV	**	**
	E - Gorges de Boltana	7	II - III	**	**
	Forcos	5	III - IV (5) (x)	**	**

*** = Outstanding
** = Recommended
* = Limited interest

Spanish Rivers

River Basin	River	km	Difficulty	WW stars	Scenery
Río Cinca	Cinca A - upper	5	IV (D)	**	**
	B - lower	14	II - III (4) D	**	**
	Cinqueta A - high	2.5	V - VI (xx)	***	***
	B - upper	2	V - V+	**	***
	C - Red Gorges	0.8	V (6) E	***	***
	D - Classic	4	IV - V (x)	***	***
	E - lower	3.5	IV - V (x) E	***	**
	Aso	1.5	IV - V (xx) E	**	**
	Barrosa	9	IV - V (6) D	***	**
	Irues	5	IV (5) (x) E	***	***
Río Esera	Esera	20	III - IV (5) E D	**	**
	Vallibierna	6.5	V - VI (x) E	***	**
	Estos	5	IV - V	***	***
	Barranco de Viú	6	IV - V (5+) (6) E	**	**
	Barbaruens	4	IV - V (xx) E	**	***
	Barranco de Ilert	9	III - IV	*	**
	Isabeña A - upper	4	IV - V	**	**
	B - from Monastere	10	IV - V D	**	**
Río Noguera Ribagorçana	Baliera A - upper	5	V - VI (xxx) E D	*	**
	B - lower	5	IV - V (6) (x) E	**	**
	Noguera de Tor A - upper	2.5	IV (5+)	**	**
	B - middle	7	III (4) (x)	**	**
	C - lower	8.5	III - IV	**	**
Río Noguera Pallaresa	Noguera Pallaresa A - high	13	III - IV (5) E	**	***
	B - upper	14	IV - V	***	***
	C - from Escalo	8	II	**	*
	D - Classic	35	III - IV+ D	***	**
	Caregue (or Berasti)	4	IV+ D	**	*
	Lladorre	1	III (4)	**	***
	Noguera de Vallferrera	4	IV - IV E	***	***
	Noguera de Tor	4.5	IV+	**	**
	Santa Magdalena	10	IV - V D	**	**
	Manyanet	4	IV -V -VI (xxx) E	**	**
	Bellera	8	III - IV (5)	**	*
Río Segre	Segre A - upper	9.5	II - III - IV (5)	**	*
	B - lower	10	II - III	**	*
	Le Carol	9.5	IV (5) (6) D	**	**
	Lavansa	8	IV - V (xx) E+	*	***
	Río Valira Del Nord	11	IV - V (5+)	**	*

Publisher's Note

After we published our Alps Guide Books several paddlers suggested that we should produce one for the Pyrenees. I made a quick reconnaissance there in 1998, had a great week of paddling and was pleasantly surprised with the diversity and especially at the amount of easier class 3 water.

However, our little group was totally frustrated at the lack of any kind of a guidebook: we drove many unnecessary miles scouting rivers that proved un-runnable, and we came away totally convinced of the need for one - but our hard-nosed Finance Director questioned the economics. So the book lay dormant, on that list of 'possibles' until early this year when I received a copy of the new 'Pyrénées Rivières Sauvages' written by Patrick Santal and a team of enthusiastic local paddlers. Here was the bang up-to-date guidebook that was so sorely needed - we then talked to Patrick Santal and negotiated to buy the English rights.

Any guidebook is a compromise of what is put in and what is left out and this is even more true of a translation from another language. We have tried to keep this book faithful to the author's French edition, without adding a lot of 'padding', so good or bad, **it is quite different to our other guidebooks!** We have made some minor changes in the layout, and added a few introductory sections, but the main part of the book is we hope a fairly true translation from the French - with many thanks to Norman Taylor and family for their hard work!

We would welcome contributions and suggestions for the next edition - any significant contribution receives a free book and an honorary mention.

I hope you enjoy this book, and that you have some great times paddling in the Pyrenees.

Peter Knowles, Rivers Publishing, England.

Gave de Gavarnie, "parcours E".

Foreword

You will see that the river descriptions in this book are deliberately brief. We wanted to leave you the buzz of discovery and it seemed more important to us to give you a good description of the put in and take out points and the general character of the river rather than trying to give kilometre by kilometre description of each river.

The information in this book should always be treated only as a guide, and the authors cannot be held responsible for any changes or mistakes. Any river can change in character very quickly due to fluctuations in water levels, but also due to new weirs, bridges, road widening, etc.

Every kayaker must take responsibility for their own safety. Every time you paddle a river it's a first descent!

On your river journey you will discover many places of great beauty - usually free of all pollution. The people who live in the Pyrenees and use its rivers, especially the fishermen, are committed to protecting the wonderful heritage provided by the rivers and the surrounding countryside. We ask that all kayakers should respect both the environment and the local people so that we can help protect these beautiful rivers and strengthen the sport we love.

Patrick Santal, Association. Rivières Sauvages, France.

How to use this Guide

Introduction

This book covers most navigable rivers in the Pyrenees but does not include every river. Readers can be reassured that there are probably still some rivers in the Pyrenees waiting to be discovered!!!

We have grouped the river descriptions by basin, or by large river system so that this guide is organised geographically.

At the beginning of each basin you will find a place map listing the navigable rivers with their grades. These maps are not to scale and do not give precise access and take-out points.

We have given access and take-out points that seemed the most suitable to us, but no doubt you will sometimes choose different options when you are there.

River Grading

The International Classification of Difficulty ranges from class I to the un-runnable.

Class I: moving water with almost no gradient and few or no obstacles.

Class II: paddling is still easy, small regular waves with no need for a spray deck.

Class III: manoeuvring required to avoid obstacles. Even though the fall is slightly more sustained inspection of rapids from the bank is not normally required. Spray decks are essential.

Class IV: rapids are more turbulent and sustained concentration is required to avoid obstacles. Negotiating some of the water hazards such as holes requires great caution.

Class V: inspection of the rapids from the bank is essential. These can be very steep and rocky. The rapids are very violent and often continuous. Swimming is not advisable.

Class VI: extremely difficult and can only be paddled with absolute care at precisely the right water level. Very careful inspection is essential together with safety cover from the bank.

(x) =   **Portage - t**he rapids cannot normally be paddled without extreme hazard to life.
(e.g. falls of 40 metres of more, siphons.)

Roman numerals are used to indicate the total section and

Arabic numerals in brackets are used to designate a single rapid or a very short section of the run.

For example: '3 kilometres of class IV (5)'
- This designates a river with mostly class IV rapids plus one or two class 5 rapids.

'D' = Dam. The presence of these dams is referred to in the river description.
The grades given for a river or a section do not take into account artificial structures (dams, weirs, , etc.).

'E' = committing - the river is difficult to access and take-out points are rare and almost non- existent.(think of a faint despairing cry for "..elp" from the bottom of some deep gorge! = French 'engage')

Water Levels

All grades are given for a water level consistent with a medium flow. It must be borne in mind that greater than normal water levels will mean a higher class than those given.

In some cases, where it was possible, we have given you some measure of water level by means of a gauge. We repeat, however, that this is only a guide (erosion of the river bed can change the readings on a gauge from one season to another). (We have used the abbreviation 'cumecs' = cubic metres per second)

Conversions

100 cumecs is roughly 3500 cfs.   5 miles = 8 km.
A gradient of 10 metres per km is roughly 50 ft a mile.

When to paddle

The rivers of the Pyrenees are for the most part not big rivers with a strong flow. On the contrary most flow along at the bottom of narrow valleys with a variable but regular gradient.

Most paddling usually takes place during the snow melt from the beginning of April to May-June. The bulk of the thaw starts earlier in Spain (from mid-April to the start of June depending on snow fall for the year) than in France (mid-May to the end of June).

It is also possible to paddle after rainfall but this is of course more chancy. The western side of the Pyrenees (the Basque country, Bearn, Navarre) has a more predictable rainfall than the other regions, in Autumn and during the Winter.

Note that it is usually possible to paddle the larger rivers like the Noguera Pallaresa all year round.

Which boat to use

For the more difficult rivers with the most testing sections (littered with rocks and a steep gradient) kayaks with rounded ends are preferable to flat pointed boats.

Even though traditionally most of the rivers have been run with long, high volume boats, passage of time and the development of new materials has established that it is better to use relatively short kayaks on sections of class IV and above. Below this grade choice of craft is not really important since the rivers are wider and less technical.

Patrick Santal

The high performance 'skinny' kayaks popped through
the syphons with ease - their overweight occupants however
did not have such an easy time...

Kayaking in the Pyrenees

The Pyrenees

The Pyrenees offer a varied environment overriding their geographical uniformity. The diversity of climatic effects together with the complex geology has created a truly patchwork landscape.

From the high mountain peaks and green shady valleys of Ariege, to the smoothness of the rounded Basque hills and the luminous yellow dryness of parts of the countryside in Aragon or Catalan, Nature gives us so many opportunities to marvel and escape. For here, although Nature is in control everywhere she has kept her soul, wild and intimate - if sometimes severe - encouraging us to discover it.

The Pyrenees also consists of a spectrum of still flourishing cultures. Even though we are just passing through and white water is the ultimate aim of our visit, it remains essential to know how to appreciate such culture - ruins, buildings, the cuisine, traditional skills and activities all bear witness to a rich and ancient history.

Leisure sports form an integral part of the new life styles, creating an important base for the stable economic development of the valleys. Mountaineering, skiing, caving, climbing, kayaking, hang gliding, canyoning and all the new white water sports have found a natural home here in the Pyrenees.

This combination of ancient culture and modern outdoor eco-tourism generates an intimate, laid back and genuine atmosphere that gives quality of life that is difficult to match. And a kayaking holiday undoubtedly provides a marvellous way of experiencing the Pyrenees.

The Rivers

A guide book to the Pyrenees quotes *'a huge castle of clouds and water feeds the neighbouring plains with many powerful torrents interrupted by the waterfalls that form one of the dramatic visual and resounding features of the Pyrenees...'* The variety of the landscape described above is the origin of the very diverse profusion of rivers.

About **120 navigable rivers** can be counted from East to West and from North to South. If you relate this number to the surface area of the mountain chain and its surroundings you become aware of the closeness of one river to another.

This lavishness shows even more in the sheer diversity of the rivers. Contrasts in relief and vegetation create characteristic river profiles:

- **narrow gorges** hemmed in by massive limestone cliffs (Rioumajou, Neste d'Aure, the Salazar...),
- **rushing torrents** of the heights (Gavarnie, Cauterets, Cinqueta, Vallferrera...),
- **bigger deeper rivers** (Gallego, Grande Nive, Gorges of Ossau and Aspa, Garonne, the Cinca, Noguera Pallaresa...) of the Piedmont.

The varied **climate** makes for very specific conditions when paddling. To the West the low relief and proximity to sea level gives the rivers a predominantly pluvial aspect. They are paddled in Autumn or at the beginning of Spring when rainfall is heavy and plentiful. Elsewhere river types are more mixed, their different characteristics always varying according to the slopes. To the South the thaw is obviously earlier than in the North. You can paddle the Ara in April-May but you can brave the gorge of Cauterets up until July, even August in some years. The southern slopes get the benefit of lots of sunshine in the Spring and the temperature quickly becomes pleasant from April-May while you can still be complaining that your fingers are numbed with cold in Ariege or Bearn. The climate to the West of the massif is also gentler than to the East of Pau.

Making use of all these factors means that you can paddle in the Pyrenees all the year round.

The Kayaking

Everyone, depending on their skill, their mood and their motivation can paddle the rivers of the Pyrenees.

The **middle or lower sections** of the rivers (grade II, III, (4)) lend themselves easily to an introduction to the water, to recreational paddling or to playing on the waves: the Grande Nive, the Gallego, the classic Larrau, the gorges of the Aspe and the Ossau, the Haut-Adour, the Esera etc...

Elsewhere you can launch yourself into the rapids, shoot the drops, and wrestle with the river hazards in optimum conditions of safety: proximity of a road, medium water level, lots of available information, accessible location: St Engrace, Haut-Larrau (where every year at the beginning of April the build up of the Haute Soule takes place) and also Brousset, Ouzom, Lourdios, Haut-Aspe, Gavarnie etc...

For the more **adventurous** there are many other rivers to satisfy the challenge of the unknown places, farther, deeper, more committing. Spain is revealed as a land of wonderful adventure. You search for put in points at the end of interminable, indistinct trails. This uncertainty shows itself yet again in the course of the river: with no information on river features, the group is left to its own judgement, skill and capability.

If these ingredients of discovery, uncertainty, isolation, and commitment are what you are looking for then the large watersheds of the Spanish slopes: the Aragon, Cinca, Esera, Noguera Pallaresa are fed by wild tributaries that few paddlers have attempted.

On the French side one could explore the bottom of sometimes hostile gorges to experience the same commitment, examples such as the Heas, or the Haute St Engrace.

Jean Preux

Permission for Spanish rivers

In a few Spanish provinces permission is required to paddle the rivers, notably in the province of **Aragon** where you will find several white water stretches that are absolute gems. The provinces of Navarra and Cataluna do not have the same system and here you can paddle freely.

Canoe and kayaking is not allowed during November, December and January. During April, May, June, July and August it is allowed from midday up until 18.00 hours. Paddling is unlimited during the months of February, March, September and October.

Note that **paddling is forbidden in National Parks** of Ordesa and of Mount Perdu (that would mainly affect the rivers Arazas and Vellos) or in the National Park of Aigues Tortes - on both rivers and lakes.

For the province of **Aragon**, authorisation is needed for all the tributaries of the Ebro, and the Veral (the most westerly), Ara, Cinca, up until the Baliera (the most easterly). Checks are made regularly, although not systematically, on the rivers Veral, Ara and Cinca and if you do not have permission you could be booked by the Police.

For more information and to obtain permission you should apply to:

> Confederacion Hydrografica del Ebro
> Paseo de Sagasta 24-28
> 50071 Zaragoza
> Tel: (34) 976 22 19 93

For some rivers you currently have to pay for authorisation and apply about 6 months in advance but a plan is under consideration to sell day or period permits from the beginning of 1999. For more information about this please contact the Spanish Tourism Office at Ainsa. Tel: (34) 974 50 07 67.

(Note that local rafting companies are normally knowledgeable and a friendly source of advice!)

Planning your trip

Introduction

It's not essential to do any planning: we've driven out to Europe for a long week's paddling, just thrown the boats on the car, headed off to Dover and caught the first ferry. But, many things can go wrong, and a little planning will usually give peace of mind and lead to a happier holiday.

Before you go

A little bit of time beforehand on reading and research can make your holiday a much better quality trip and save you time and money.

We suggest that spend some time on the internet, and write off, or fax for information from tourist offices in the main centres you are planning to visit and also obtain up-to-date travel information from your motoring organisation or other source. A Spanish and French phrase book will repay their cost many times over.

If you are driving from Britain, then you should check your car insurance company and extend the cover to other European countries if necessary.

Car breakdown insurance gives peace of mind but can be expensive. It's worth looking hard at the policies and doing a 'what if' scenario. If you do two or more trips a year then you should probably think about annual cover for the whole of Europe.

Medical cover

We recommend that you take out specialist medical and travel insurance for your trip to the Pyrenees. If you are involved in an accident and are injured whilst kayaking or rafting it is likely that you will incur not only hospital charges, but also ambulance transfer fees and helicopter call out fees in some cases. Serious accidents may also need subsequent air ambulance and repatriation to your home country.

Most general travel insurance policies will exclude white water rafting and kayaking as they view these as high risk and in our experience you are better talking to a specialist company such as Activecard (U.K. Tel: 01327 262805). Policies bought direct from companies like these are normally much better value than one's bought through second parties - in some parts of the travel industry the mark up on insurance can be as high as 100%. If you travel regularly then an annual multi-trip policy is well worth considering, but again, do make sure that any high risk activities are specifically covered - it should also cover you if you break your leg one weekend skiing!

European countries often have reciprocal health agreements with the U.K. A form DSS E111 (available from post offices) helps in administering medical expenses claimed back from the NHS in the U.K. and is a useful thing to have. This is particularly recommended if you choose not to take out travel insurance as it will help you claim back some of your medical expenses. But note that it is not an alternative to insurance, many hospitals and rescue services will still insist on you paying the bill or producing evidence of insurance.

Planning your programme

Pyrenees rivers may well be more powerful and challenging than those you are used to, so we urge you to be conservative in your plans:

- Don't aim to do too much paddling - **give yourself time** - remember that there are many other enjoyable things to do in this beautiful region.
- Give careful thought to your itinerary so that you **build confidence and experience on easier rivers** before progressing to the more challenging ones.
- **Be flexible** in your plans and adjust them if for example you're feeling tired or if local river conditions aren't good.

Paddlers do die on rivers and usually it's because events, or people have pressurised them to do a run, which, if they were alive to reflect on it, they should not have attempted that day.

What to take

Although the weather in the Pyrenees is often hot and sunny you should remember that some rivers are fed by snow melt water and you will need suitable equipment for paddling cold rivers, and to survive the odd swim. We recommend a long john wet suit, thermal tops, dry-top paddling jacket, and wet suit boots, besides your normal paddling equipment.

Paddling in the Pyrenees can a bit of an expedition, so your equipment should reflect the fact that you may be at the bottom of a gorge and remote from outside help - your group should be self sufficient and suitably equipped for most emergencies with first aid, safety, and rescue gear. This is a 'where to go' rather than a 'how to do it' book - if you feel you need further guidance then we recommend a practical course at a good kayak or rafting school. It's also worth packing some spare paddling gear and a repair kit.

The south of France and Spain can be very hot - up to 40 degrees - so it's worth packing the ice box, sun awning, and loose cotton clothing. Sports sandals such as Tevas are really comfortable and healthy (banish smelly trainers to the car roof!).

You will find that most foods that you can buy in your home country are available in both France and Spain and at roughly comparable prices so it usually makes little financial sense to load your car down with food from home - you will eat much better if you buy fresh local produce, and this is surely one of the pleasures of a foreign holiday? You might want to consider though a stock of your favourite breakfast cereal and any other favourite speciality food: Brits will probably want to take fresh tea bags; Australians, vegemite; and Americans, peanut butter.

Security

Local people in the mountains are honest and hard-working and in our experience you are less likely to have anything stolen than in your own home city, however you are on holiday so it does pay to take basic precautions - particularly when in or near to cities:

- Leave valuables in the safe keeping of your hotel or campsite guardian.

- Photocopy important documents (e.g. passport) and keep these separate.

- Take important phone numbers and money with you on the river in a waterproof pouch on your person.

- Take two cable locks so that you can lock boats both to your roof rack and if you leave any at your campsite.

(The worst incident we have heard of was some paddlers who left their car in the South of France with everything in it and returned to find it had been stolen. The car had contained all their possessions, so they were left standing by the roadside in their swim trunks, with no money, no clothes, no friends and no papers - the despairing cry 'mother' echoed up the lonely valley!)

Flying to Europe

Flying with rafts and inflatable kayaks from North America is relatively straight-forward, but many airlines don't like plastic kayaks and will try to charge you air cargo rates if you contact them in advance. Best thing is probably to phone and ask them in advance if they take surf boards, and provided they do, turn up on the day to check in with your 'surf kayak'. Some airlines will waive excess charges if you only check in one bag - a long thin plastic one!

When you're considering which airline to fly with, our experience is that some of the less famous airlines try harder. Air India actually promotes itself as 'the kayak friendly airline'! However, note that KLM have a hard nosed policy of no kayaks, surf boards, wind surfers, cycles, or any other kind of adult fun toy. It's normally easier flying boats back from Europe to the States than vice versa, so you may want to consider the idea of buying a kayak to take back with you.

On flights from the U.K. there are some very cheap charter flights into airports like Bilbao, Biarritz, and Carcasonne, but these no-frills airlines have a strict scale of charges for excess luggage.

It is perfectly feasible to fly in, hire a car and a boat and go from there - you can hire boats from one of the kayak schools or shops that advertise in this book - most speak good English. The biggest problem you are likely to encounter is that very few hire companies have roof racks. If you only have one of two boats then the simple solution (in our limited experience and without prejudice) is to just tie them flat on the roof of the car with some padding as protection.

Driving from the U.K.

Getting to the Pyrenees from the UK involves a simple, if somewhat tedious journey across France. From the French channel ports it's about a 10-12 hour drive to the French side of the Pyrenees and then, say to Sort, another 1 1/2 to 2 hours over the mountains from Montréjeau. If you've time to kill and want a more relaxing journey you could take the ferry from Portsmouth to Bilbao (which takes some 30hours) but this is really only worthwhile if you're intending paddling the western end of the Pyrenees.

If you have 2 or 3 drivers then it's worth considering cruising the motorways through the night - we recommend that you leave room in the car so that you can stretch out when not driving. We normally switch drivers every two hours so that the driver is always fresh, and stop for coffee, toilet and petrol every four hours. If you only have one driver, or a fractious family, then you might want to make an overnight break. If you have a choice of vehicle, remember that in most of Europe, diesel fuel is a lot cheaper than petrol.

The different channel crossings all have their pros and cons. The ferry companies naturally want you to book in advance, but in our experience, unless it's a bank holiday, you can normally just drive up at Dover or Folkestone and get on the next ferry or train. On the longer routes, for example to Bilbao you need to book well in advance. These longer routes can save a lot of driving time and mean that you arrive relatively fresh.

Driving in Europe

That the mainland Europeans drive on the right hand side of the road probably goes without saying. However, they do have a few other little quirks which are not so obvious. The main one is that traffic coming from the right has right of way. The exceptions to this are: round-a-bouts, motorways, and most main roads which are then marked as priority roads. This means that at all other times i.e. when there are no signs and no road markings you must **give way to the right**.

There are also a few other legal requirements. These vary from country to country but generally:

- You must carry your driving licence at all times when driving.

- You should carry a warning triangle and first aid kit in the car at all times.

- You must carry your vehicle registration document together with your insurance certificate. It is also advisable to carry a European Accident Statement which is normally supplied by your insurer.

Failure to observe any of these requirements can result in a hefty, on the spot fine!

Peter Knowles

Notes on Countries

FRANCE

Rivers elsewhere

France is a large country and has a huge number of rivers suitable for canoeing, kayaking, and rafting - some 700 according to one guidebook. The French **Alps** is the most popular region for the white water enthusiast (see our guide book *'White Water Europe - South Alps'*) however the rivers of the **Central Massif** offer an alternative for the paddler looking for easier rivers - famous names are the Tarn, Lot, Ardèche, and the Allier.

There is usually some good **surf** to be had on the Atlantic beaches north of Biarritz.

Language

The French are proud of their language and culture so naturally they appreciate you attempting to use it, but these days all young people learn English at school and seem happy to practice it.

We visited and spoke to quite a lot of tourist information centres and all had staff who spoke good English. Most rafting centres and kayak centres also had one member of staff who spoke some English - generally someone who had paddled in New Zealand, Nepal, or North America.

Money

As a rough guide, French Francs were about 9 to the pound, and 6 to the dollar at the time of writing, but expect this to change.

You might as well forget about bringing travellers cheques - the French just love their Visa Cards and it has become a nation that is almost more credit card friendly than North America. You will need cash for the occasional drink or campsite fee but this is easily obtained from a cash dispenser as long as you know your PIN number (or even over the counter at larger banks).

Food and Drink

France has its pizza, 'pomme frites' and MacDonald's. This is a country, however, which is still proud of its heritage of good food. Lorry drivers will sit down to a four course lunch at a 'Routiers' restaurant (worth looking out for) and French housewives still walk to the local market to buy their fresh produce. When in France, we recommend that you do as the French: have lots of barbecues and picnic style meals with salads and locally grown, fresh produce.

We suggest that you try to do most of your shopping in local markets and small shops rather than bland supermarkets as it's lots more fun, the food is much better, with superb flavoured quality produce, and remember, you will be both inter-acting with, and supporting local people. A Boulangerie is a bread shop, and a Patisserie is a fancy cake shop that often makes its own choco-lates and ice cream - don't let anyone loose in here with the team kitty! A Charcuterie is a pork butcher, but often more of a delicatessen, with freshly roasted chickens, pies, hams and sausages, freshly made salads, and mouth-watering quiches - great for picnic lunches or suppers - well, after a few bottles of wine, who feels like cooking?

Traditional, family-run restaurants usually serve delicious local cooking and in our experience offer excellent value - best is the 'table d'hote' fixed price meal. Sadly, after two weeks of all this temptation and good food, one vegetarian friend of ours succumbed and reverted to being a carnivore!

Driving

French roads are generally good and it's almost a pleasure to drive on their motorways. Short sections of motorway around the larger cities are usually free, but other motorways have toll charges that can be quite expensive, depending on your budget and the number in your vehicle. Main trunk roads, called 'Route National' (RN) have improved considerably in the last few years and are worth considering if you are on a budget and have plenty of time as they take you through all those interesting old towns and villages. Minor roads are often bumpy and poorly marked so night driving on these can be as exciting as class IV!

Camping

French campsites are numerous, and good value. Most have hot showers and a wide variety of facilities. All are graded from one to five stars. Typically in 1999 we were paying about £2.50 per head per night on a three star site. Some of the smaller, more attractive sites do get fully booked in the main summer holiday period (August) but there are usually plenty of other local sites. If you like the idea of camping, but don't want the hassle of carrying and setting up tents, then a few companies such as 'Eurocamp' have fixed tents set up on campsites in some of the centres. These can be good value outside the school holiday period.

An alternative to camping, especially worth considering earlier in the season are **'Gite d'Etaps'** which are small independent hostels that have to satisfy national standards. Typical price for a bed for the night is around £7 and many have twin bed rooms. These are great places for meeting and socialising with outdoor-orientated French people, food is usually substantial and often excellent. Another idea for early in the season is to hire a holiday apartment in one of the ski resorts which at this time of year can be almost cheaper than camping. Local tourist offices will help you make a booking if you need help.

Peter Knowles.

SPAIN

Introduction

Spain is made up of a number of autonomous regions. Usually this would be a matter of supreme indifference to the majority of paddlers but access to rivers and any necessary permits are aspects that are controlled by local government organisations. See the notes on access elsewhere in this guide.

Notwithstanding the need or not for permits large groups should be particularly aware that local rafting and guiding companies are becoming increasingly more protective of their "turf" - and will report to the civil guard groups operating in what could be seen as a commercial manner.

It's good advice to take a form **E111** which will simplify matters if you need to make use of medical facilities in Spain. 112 is the telephone number for the emergency services. 91 is the national number for the police.

Rivers Elsewhere

There is some excellent paddling to be had in Gallicia which is a delightfully undiscovered region in the North West of Spain on the border with Portugal - at it's best in Spring and Autumn. The excellent guidebook *'Kayak en Galicia'* by Andres Gonzalez gives more information.

Please see the next section for details of paddling rivers on the North Coast of Spain and the Rio Ebro.

Language

As you would expect most Spaniards speak Spanish! This truism is not necessarily as daft as it sounds as Castilian Spanish (in which you might have a rusty O-level) might not necessarily be a local's first language. In the Pyrenees you will come across two other languages Basque (in the West) and Catalan (in the East) while north of Portugal you will find locals speaking Gallego.

Basque (or Euskera) is the oldest language still in use in Europe and is spoken on both sides of the Pyrenees. **Catalan** clearly is spoken mainly in Cataluña. As a visitor to Spain it is likely that any efforts that you can make in "castellano" will be much appreciated. However expect to overhear the other languages and be aware that road signs use both Castilian and either Basque or Catalan as appropriate.

Money

The Spanish currency is the **peseta.** At the time of writing there are an astonishing 270 pesetas to the pound or 175 to the dollar. A more normal exchange rate would be around 250 pesetas to the pound. Credit cards are becoming much more widely accepted but you'd be well advised not to always rely on these particularly if you're travelling off the beaten track.

It's intended that the **Euro** will start circulation in January 2002 and the peseta will then be withdrawn.

Food and Drink

This subject deserves a whole book not just a short section!

If you insist, you can feed yourself very cheaply. Larger towns will have a "supermercado" with a wide range of foodstuffs that you can load in your trolley. In smaller villages there might be the just the one shop that stocks everything - these are not usually self-service so take a phrase book. Most shops close at luchtime - which actually means from 1.00pm to 4.00pm!

Eating out, on the other hand is to be highly recommended and much cheaper than in the U.K. Many restaurants will have a "Menu del Dia" which can offer 3 courses, bread and wine for less than the meanest paddler would pay in a Little Chef and it'll be a lot tastier. Everywhere will have their specialities "tipico de la region" - well worth trying. Be warned that the Spanish do eat much later than we're used to, most restaurants not opening until 9.00pm or later.

Driving

When driving in Spain it is compulsory to carry your driving licence (all sections), the vehicle logbook and insurance documents. Check with your insurance company for the latest information on green cards and bail-bonds. You are also expected to carry two warning triangles, spare bulbs and fuses. Drivers who wear glasses need to carry a spare pair with them at all times when driving. Bizarrely it is illegal both to carry spare fuel and to run out! Impoverished paddlers driving a heap should also be aware that it's illegal to tow or be towed by another vehicle.

Petrol prices are, on the whole, cheaper than the in U.K. Choose from Super, Normal, Sin plomo (lead free) and Gasoleo (diesel).

Traffic offences usually carry a fine with foreigners being issued on the spot fines. In proper paddling tradition though you qualify for a 20% discount for fines paid on the spot.

Accommodation

Most campsites in Spain tend to be quite plush affairs and charge accordingly. Charges are often made per tent so if you roll up with lots of small tents the bill will be disproportionately large. To rent a house or apartment on the other hand is comparatively economical, particularly out of season. The local tourist office is a useful source of contacts.

According to the 'Rough Guide to the Pyrenees' camping outside campsites is legal - but with certain exceptions: in urban areas, tourist zones, National Parks, etc. There are obvious security problems with leaving a tent unattended, but you are probably not likely to be harassed if you find a discrete 'doss spot' for the night.

Other options include lots of reasonably priced hotels, "hostales" and "residencias". The latter two are usually the cheapest option. They are all required to display a price list in the lobby so you can easily check if your Spanish is limited. Prices are usually for two people sharing a room. Breakfast is usually extra.

Phil Quil

The North Coast of Spain

Introduction

Surprisingly close to the coast and about 90km west of Santander are **Los Picos de Europa**. These spectacular limestone mountains have peaks exceeding 2,600metres whose snow covered tops served as landmarks to sailors in times gone by. The area is popular with the Spanish, particularly in August but is otherwise comparatively little known and remains one of the few genuinely unspoilt areas of Europe. Although given the rate at which new roads are being built (with EC money) don't wait too long.

The mountains have been eroded by three main rivers the Cares, Sella and Deva resulting in impressively deep gargagantas (or gorges).

The north of Spain has always had a well-deserved reputation for its rainy climate (not all the rain in Spain falls mainly on the plain!) but even so the coastline between Ribadesella and Unquera enjoys a special microclimate that allows the growth of oranges and avocados. However all this rain means that water levels zoom up and down - early spring probably offers the most reliable water levels when rainfall coincides with snowmelt higher up.

The Rio Sella

The Rio Sella is well known to marathon paddlers with the annual race from Arriondas to Ribadesella a must-do event held on the first weekend of August each year. For white water paddlers it's the upper sections above Cangas de Onis that provide greater interest. Downstream from the junction with the Rio Ponga there's lots of entertaining grade 3 while above the Ponga there's one particularly notable grade 4 squeeze which is worthy of inspection. On a good day with lots of rain the Ponga is a short but sweet diversion.

The Cares Gorge

If you're in the area of the Picos do make sure that you allow a day to walk the Cares gorge but try do avoid weekends and the holiday month of August when it can get unbearably crowded (at other times you can have it largely to yourself). This path literally cuts its way through the cliff face high above the river resulting in an easy walk but in a spectacular setting. If you can face the look down there's excellent views of the unfortunately off-limits river and lots of opportunity for if-only route finding.

The middle Cares from just below Puente Poncebos with a half decent flow has several kilometres of grade 4-5. Below Areñas de Cabrales the river is fed from a hydro scheme and creates a reliable 10 kilometre section of river that is a true classic run. Superb scenery and hugely enjoyable grade 3 - 3+ water (But... see the note below regarding permits). Below this the river is still very pretty but less exciting in white water terms.

The Rio Deva

The Rio Deva pretty well marks the eastern extent of the Picos mountains with the start of the grade 2 - 4 section starting just inside the Cantabrian regional boundary. The sting is at the start and it then settles down to a very pleasant grade 2-3. Once the Deva joins the Cares it pretty well flattens out otherwise there's a fair bit of grade 5+ above this section if you're game! All three rivers are easily inspected with roads running alongside.

Access and Permits

These superb rivers also sustain a fair population of Salmon. And we all know what that means.... Fishermen! Like every other region in Europe, salmon numbers are on the decline. Unlike every other regions in Europe where drift-nets are largely held responsible here they prefer to blame the poor innocent, fish-friendly paddler. In recent years this has resulted in the need for permits which you can obtain from Confederación Hidrografica del Norte, Comisaria de Aguas, Oficinas Centrales, Plaza de España, 2-33071 - Oviedo.

The permits come with a number of "limitaciones" - each year these have got steadily more restrictive to the extent that some river sections (including some of those mentioned above) are out of bounds for part or all of the year. Hopefully this outrageous situation will ease as the authorities realise that fishing isn't the only "turismo activo" to bring money into the area.

The current access situation effectively means for British paddlers that it's a long way to go for not a lot of paddling but stopping off on your way to Galicia or perhaps combining a family or walking holiday with a river or two would make the journey much more worthwhile. Brittany Ferries run a service from Plymouth to Santander or P&O go from Portsmouth to Bilbao.

Surfing and sea kayaking

Other attractions in the area include some superb surf beaches. Particularly notable are Playa de San Antolin west of Llanes, the beach at Ribadesella and the nearby Playa de Vega. Also highly recommended would be a spot of sea kayaking. The coastline has an almost infinite number of coves, caves, blowholes and islands waiting to be explored but don't forget the Biscay's reputation - check the weather forecast and sea state first!

Accommodation and food

Most campsites in the area are located on the coast although there are others inland near Cangas, Areñas de Cabrales and Arriondas. They tend to be quite large, plush affairs and most of them are only open over the summer months. Certainly if your going out of season renting a house is a highly recommended alternative and excellent value. The Spanish Tourist Office (0171 486 8077) can provide a "Guia de Campings" and a "Guia de Casa de Aldea" for Asturias which will give you more choice than you can cope with.

For the cultured there's an abundance of historical architecture particularly pre-romanesque and romanesque and any number of caves with paintings and other signs of paleolithic art. For the not so cultured try out your cider pouring skills but do put on your dry cag first. Cultured or not - eat out lots. Restaurants are cheap (ask for the Menu del Día if your feeling particularly thrifty) and the food is sensational. Fabada, bogavante and cabrito are particularly recommended. Don't miss out on some cabrales cheese and for those with a sweet tooth arroz con leche is a speciality of the area.

Phil Quil

Río Ebro

This major river has it's source very close to **Santander** but flows South East to collect the rivers of the Spanish Pyrenees as its tributaries. It has two notable sections that are rafted, the first is the Arroyo section below where the river runs out from the reservoir **Embalse del Ebro**.

SECTION A - about 12 km of class III

Follow the road out of the village of **Arroyo** on the right hand bank of the river for about one mile until you reach a grass parking area right beside the river, it is the first obvious access to the river that you will come across so it is impossible to miss. Take out is possible at any of the bridges across the section as the road follows the valley crossing the river occasionally. Immediately after the third bridge on the left hand side is where the rafting trips finish, although it is possible to continue although the river becomes more and more congested by trees.

The rapids on this stretch are all interspersed by flat sections and the routes are all obvious from the water. There are a few forbidding looking horizon lines but these are merely straight forward ramps up to about 20 feet long and pose no problems at all. Although there are no portages be careful of numerous trees in and overhanging the river.

After paddling this section I recommend a visit to the monastery (the large building with the big aerial set high up on the hill overlooking the river on the right hand bank) where you can get a cheap but wholesome meal and if you want to look at the monks's butterfly collection!

SECTION B ('Grand Canyon del Ebro') about 12 km of class II-III

The grand canyon of the Ebro river is not particularly challenging, as the majority of it is flat but it has some amazing views of a huge canyon similar to the Arizonian version but not quite as long or deep - but equally as impressive. This section begins above the road bridge at **Escalada** on route N623 between Santander and Burgos.

After about 100 yards a weir is shot centre right followed by a right hand bend with a large eddy on the left, begin this next section on the right hand side which continues for about 300 yards of continuous big bouncy grade three.

After this stretch there are only minor rapids and plenty of trees to look out for as the river drops steadily into the canyon with amazing views of cliffs and rock pillars on either side and vultures flying overhead.

This section ends at the **Pesquera de Ebro** after the river flows out of the canyon. At the takeout are picnic tables, a volleyball court and substantial brick barbeques so that a conscientious shuttle bunny can have a feast waiting for you! Egress is on the left hand side at the village picnic and camping area. It is possible to continue to any of the villages further downstream but the river is largely flat although great for family float trips.

Ben Love

"Damn!" - the dam workers were at lunch again...

Flora and Fauna

It would obviously be difficult for a kayaker in the action of descending a rapid to pay too much attention to the indigenous plant and animal life of to be found in a typical Pyrenee's valley.

However, when the rapids become a little calmer and the descent slower it should be easy to pick out the **Dipper** (Cinclus cinclus) in action. This bird, also known as the water blackbird, is dark with a white bib. Highly active, it can dive into the water and may spend several minutes walking along the bottom of the stream in a whirl of bubbles seeking its prey.

Even though the Pyrenean Desman (or **trumpet rat**, Galemys pyrenaicus) is very typical of the area it is rare to see this little aquatic mammal which is extremely susceptible to levels of water pollution. Often said to be confined to the Pyrenees, it has however been observed in other regions in the Iberian mountains.

A small newt, the Pyrenean Euprocte, is very typical of these mountains but lives in the upper reaches of torrents not paddled by the kayaker.

The **trout** is, of course, the most common fish found in the well oxygenated waters of the rapids. Research has shown that these fish originate from the sea. To be honest, that would be a common-place prediction from looking at the physiology: a progressive change during millions of years of time and episodes of glaciation from a saline to a fresh water environment. The common trout is the only true native of the Pyrenees. It has become progressively scarcer here and in the mountain lakes. The rainbow trout, originally from North America, has largely been used for restocking by fishing groups. Less fussy than the common trout in its feeding habits, it is also less wary.

Food for the fish is mainly provided by small invertebrates living around the waterfalls and streams. It consists essentially of insects belonging to the following families: beetles, mayflies, caddis flies (Trichoptera, whose larvae are well known for their portable cases made with sand grains or plant fragments), dragonflies etc....

Their relative abundance depends on the amount of sunshine, the temperature of the water, the type of banks, nature of the vegetation, degree of oxygenation of the water and, of course, the time of year. The life cycle of all these insects and its effect on the development of the young trout has been the subject of much agronomical research in the Pyrenees by the INRA of the Basque country and by the Universities of Toulouse and Montpellier.

The **rapids** form a distinct world of their own, a special ecological community where tenuous links form connections between the plants of the river itself (microscopic such as diatamous algae or macroscopic like the flowering plants seen more easily in the flow of water), the plants on the river banks, herbivorous insects, carnivorous insects and other invertebrates and, finally, the fish. This aquatic environment is also dependant on the countryside which surrounds it. The level of **pollution** is easily discerned in the vegetation of the river and its banks - a bloom of yellowish algae indicates high levels of nitrates of agricultural origin whereas an abundance of the Royal Fern (Osmonda regalis, the largest of the European ferns) is a sure sign that the waters are clean and healthy.

On the northern slopes of the western Pyrenees, large colonies of Polygonum (Japanese Knotweed) demonstrate that sometimes a species foreign to the region (termed adventitious by the botanists) can flourish. This example emphasises the fragility of the living community of plants and animals in these streams and rivers and that many factors, both human and otherwise, planned or accidental, can cause rapid change. Such fragility calls for care from the various users of the rivers: not only those who, by irresponsible application of industry, agriculture or urbanisation could greatly alter their ecology, but also those who enjoy white water sport.

C. Dendaletche, Pyreneean naturalist

Hydrology

The rate of flow of the mountain rivers in the Pyrenees depends on several factors; water releases from dams, rainfall and melting of the snows. Although the first factor can be controlled, the other two depend on the whims of nature. So what are usual effects of these?

Rainfall

The mountains can be divided for simplicity into two areas:

- The first is the **Atlantic region** taking in the Spanish Basque country, the Aran valley and all the French slopes of the Atlantic Pyrenees up to Ariege.
- The second area, the **Mediterranean part**, takes in all the other Spanish slopes, Andorra and the Eastern Pyrenees.

The rainfall differs in these two regions. On the **Atlantic slopes** rainfall is plentiful, from 1 metre a year around Ariege to 1.50 metres in the West and up to 2 metres a year in the Basque country. The rains are fairly well differentiated between a wet Winter and, particularly, Spring and a drier Summer and Autumn. It rains just about twice as much in the wettest month of May than in July, the driest.

However, during the Summer the rains are bought in by air currents largely caused by winds from the South-West, the West and the North-West. These currents give rise to wide spread rain that swells the rapids, especially the main ones of the lower valleys. The high mountain peaks present a barrier to these air currents, producing an effect whereby the north-west wind brings rain to the French side but not the Spanish and vice versa with a south-west wind. Air currents from the West cause rainfall mainly in the Atlantic Pyrenees.

Some rainfall however manages to cross over the mountain ridge and in this way stormy weather from the South-West lasting several days can end up causing heavy rain on the French side at Gavarnie and flooding of the Gave at Lourdes.

On the **Mediterranean slopes** the rainfall is weaker, from 0.5 to 1 metre a year, with a slightly different distribution. The two Summer months are the driest and Autumn is the wettest season. The ratio of the rainfall between the driest month of July and the wettest, October, is 1 to 4. Another characteristic is that the number of days with heavy rainfall are definitely lower: it rains less often - but when it does, it really rains!

Storms

These occur almost exclusively from May to September, on average for 30 days a year over the whole mountain chain. They are generally the product of air currents caused by South-West winds and are moved along by these to bring rain to one slope after another. In doing so, they temporarily swell small water courses although as a whole the main torrents of the lower valleys are not particularly affected.

Depending upon the prevailing conditions, storms can persist for some time in one location and, if the rainfall is sustained, the small torrents become hugely swollen and even the main water courses in the low valleys can overflow. This rarely happens and then mainly on the Mediterranean slopes. In general storms occur almost exclusively **in the afternoons after 1 pm.**

Snow melt

The second source of water for the torrents, melt water, is easier to cope with. The main time for its production in the high mountains is in the Spring. In the depths of Winter there is almost no thawing even when the temperatures are relatively mild. This is because the sun is low in the sky, length of daylight is short and, in contrast, the long hours of darkness allow re-freezing of the snow.

At lower altitudes and on the southern slopes there is greater thawing as Winter proceeds. Above 1800 metres snowfalls typically pile up steadily from the beginning of December until March or April, the amount varying from year to year but the average total being the same for all the Winter months.

Geographically the **snowfall** can be very variable but mainly fits into the two climatic zones mentioned previously. In the northern Atlantic zone the depth of snow is consistent even though some Winters like those of 89/90 are still famous for their lack of snow cover. In contrast, variability of depth of snow is much more marked in the Mediterranean southern zone.

The process of thawing gets under way from about the beginning of April, usually from the end of March at 1800 metres and towards the end of April around 2500 metres. The thaw starts because the sun climbs higher and higher above the horizon, shines for a longer and longer time and the nights are correspondingly shorter for re-freezing the snow. The sun starts to heat up the eastern and western slopes significantly and gradually the northern slopes until finally the snow, wasted and soiled, ceases to reflect the radiance of the sun.

All these factors cause the thaw to carry on until the Spring time. During the thaw period the snow is reduced by up to 5 centimetres a day, the equivalent of 20 millimetres of rain. This corresponds to a heavy downpour - a really good storm. The thaw differs from a storm in that it acts on all the slopes at the same time, swelling quite a number of torrents that combine to cause flooding of the main torrents. By the **end of June** the thaw usually finishes at 2500 metres although the melting continues at higher altitudes at a lower rate.

The thaw varies considerably from one year to another. So around the 10 years between 84 and 94 there was a difference of one month for the end of the thaw between the more snowy and less snowy winters. When the weather is overcast and rainy during Spring the thaw largely ceases even if it is mild. The **effect of the sun** on the thaw is the dominating factor above that of ambient temperature and well above the effect of any heat coming up from the ground, which is the equivalent of only 1% of the sun's energy.

D. Vrecourt, Nivologist.

"They always make it look so difficult"

Rafting

Introduction

White water rafting was almost unknown in Europe ten years ago - now it's a multi-million pound tourist industry with over a million client trips a year.

There is a surprising selection of rafting runs in the Pyrenees as can be seen from the list below, from the scenic float trip to an aquatic bob sleigh ride. Most commercial rafting trips are offered as half day adventures to general holiday makers, but there is scope here for an enjoyable specialist rafting holiday. Your choice of river will depend on the time of year and the river flows - as in kayaking, the general advice is that the rivers on the French side are only at their best in late Spring and early summer.

Both France and Spain regulate commercial rafting and all companies and guides must be licensed. This in theory does not apply to private rafts but you may well run into difficulty with over zealous local police.

Rafting Rivers

France :

lla Nive	Gave d'Oloron	Gave d'Aspe	Gave d'Ossau
Gave de Pau	Gave de Gavarnie	l'Adour	la Neste
lla Garonne	l'Ariege	l'Aude	

Spain

Esca	Gallego	Ara	Cinca
Noguera Pallaresa	Ebro		

Rafts

Almost all the rafting in the Pyrenees is paddle rafting using rafts varying in size from 3m to 5m long. Some companies also run smaller 'mini-rafts' which you captain yourself after suitable training.

Many companies also offer one or two person inflatable canoes called les **'Hot dogs'** (Americans call these 'duckies') that are used on the easier runs. These are great fun - a typical comment is: "I got a great buzz out of paddling my own boat!"

Hydro-speeding

'Nage en eaux vive' is a French invention and consists of swimming rivers with a special toboggan-like float to protect and support the upper body.   Your group of hydro-speeders are guided down the river like a, sinuous line of fish, with a swimming leader at the front and usually accompanied by one or two safety kayakers. You wear a thick wet suit, and heavy padding to protect the lower body and swimming flippers. If you're a reasonable swimmer with flippers then do have a go at this - you're even more intimately involved with the water than a kayaker, feel every nuance of the current, and yet (unlike kayaking) this is something you can do with almost no experience!

Peter Knowles

The hazards of paddling -

in Nepal   in the Alps   in the Pyrenees

Ulrike sur le gave de Larrau, "parcours A".

Gave d'Aydius.

Nono très efficace sur l'appui, gave du Brousset.

Bon niveau d'eau sur le gave du Brousset.

Gave de Cauterets, "Gorges basses".

BASSIN DE LA NIVE

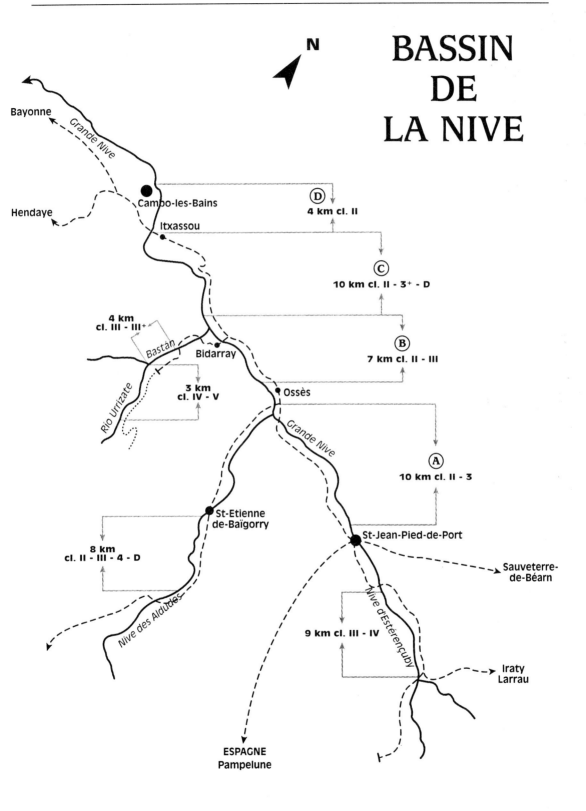

N

Bayonne

Grande Nive

Hendaye

● Cambo-les-Bains

Itxassou

Ⓓ
4 km cl. II

Ⓒ
10 km cl. II - 3⁺ - D

**4 km
cl. III - III⁺**

Bastán

● Bidarray

Ⓑ
7 km cl. II - III

Rio Urrizate

**3 km
cl. IV - V**

● Ossès

Grande Nive

Ⓐ
10 km cl. II - 3

● St-Etienne
de-Baïgorry

● St-Jean-Pied-de-Port

Sauveterre-
de-Béarn

**8 km
cl. II - III - 4 - D**

Nive des Aldudes

Nive d'Estérençuby

9 km cl. III - IV

Iraty
Larrau

ESPAGNE
Pampelune

Bassin de la Nive

Tourist Offices

BAYONNE (64100)
OFFICE DE TOURISME
Place des Basques
Tél: 05.59.46.01.46, Fax: 05.59.59.37.55

CAMBO-LES-BAINS (64250)
OFFICE DE TOURISME
Parc Public - BP 15
Tél : 05.59.29.70.25, Fax: 05.59.29.90.77

SAINT-JEAN-PIED-DE-PORT (64220)
OFFICE DE TOURISME
Place Charles de Gaulle
Tél : 05.59.37.03.57, Fax: 05.59.37.34.91

Rafting & Kayak Companies

Sensations Eaux Vives
Pierre Dentaletche
30 Allee des Acacias

64200 Biarritz
Tel: 05 59 37 78 01

Evasion Eaux Vives
Itxassou, Evasion
Cambo les Bains
Tel: 05 59 31 69

Cocktail Aventure
Residence Laminak
64310 St Pee sur Nivelle
Tel: 05 59 54 18 69
Bidarray Rafting Base
Tel: 05 59 37 76 24

UrBizia
Route Dept. 918
64780 Bidarray
Tel: 05 59 37 72 37

Twik Txak
D 933 tournant d'Ispoure
St Jean de Pied de Port
Tel: 05 59 37 12 20

La Grand Nive

The River

La Grande Nive arises from the confluence of the Nive de Valcarlos, Nive d'Esterencuby and Nive du Laurhibar. The catchment is mainly supplied by run-off rather than groundwater and levels will suffer after long periods without rain.

SECTION A (from St. Jean to St. Martin d'Arrosa)

10km of Class II (3).   Kayaking ★   Scenery ★★

Put In

Take the Cambo road (D 918) from St. Jean-Pied-de-Port and after crossing the road bridge across the Nive de Valcarlos at nearby d'Huart-Cize look out for a parking spot on the right with a path leading to the river.

Take Out

Around 10 km downstream of St. Jean-Pied-de-Port towards Cambo take the left turn (D 948) towards St. Etienne de Baigorry. This road crosses the river almost immediately and the take out is from the left bank after the bridge.

Description

Note that this section is only possible after appreciable rain. The first Class 3 rapid comes where the river bed narrows for some 100 metres. The second such rapid occurs at around half distance where the flow breaks around rocks. The remainder of the run has only minor rapids and allows enjoyment of the scenery.

SECTION B (from Osses to Bidarray)

7km of Class II-III   Kayaking ★★   Scenery ★★

Put In

Take the Cambo road (D 918) from Osses and after 800 m look out for a small metalled road on the left to reach the river. This is a cul de sac and longer term parking may be difficult.

Take Out

Around 1.7 km downstream of the left turn from the D 918 to nearby Bidarray the road and river are separated by the railway. Take out here is from the right bank eddy after the rapid by the Orhategaray Joinery workshops.

Description

There is nothing particularly difficult here. Rapids are concentrated mainly in the first two thirds of the run. After the road bridge to Bidarray a pair of Class 3 rapids enliven the approach to the take-out (see above).

You need to avoid July to September to ensure adequate water.

SECTION C   (from Biddarray to Itxassou)

10 km of Class II (3+) D   Kayaking ★   Scenery ★★

Put In
Put in at the Take out as described above.

Take Out
About 3 km after the village of **Louhossoa** take the left turn from the D 918 to nearby Itxassou. The Take out is under the arched bridge within the village.

Description
The first half of the section is Class II after which one enters the gorge known as the **'Pas de Roland'**.   After the more demanding gorge there is then a flat stretch on the approach to the barrage at Itxassou.   There is a passage for kayaks at the extreme right of the barrage.

Note that this section is **possible all year**.

SECTION D   (from Itxassou to Cambo)

4 km of Class II   Kayaking ★   Scenery ★★

Put In
At the above Get Out in Itxassou.

Take Out
Within Cambo take the road towards Hasparren and then celles des Thermes. The Take Out is at the Thermal Baths.

Description
This beautiful **all year round** run is ideal for beginners in kayak or canoe.

Rio Urrizate

3 km of Class IV-V   Kayaking ★ ★   Scenery ★ ★ ★

The River

This is a small river which starts as the Rio Urrizate in Spain and after flowing across the border into France it becomes the Bastan; to then join the Nive at **Bidarray** on the D 918. The catchment is exclusively supplied by direct run-off of rainwater and the river is free flowing with no hydro-electric dams.

Put In

Immediately after crossing the river bridge into Bidarray from the D918 turn right and shortly take the track following the Bastan upstream.. After 1.5km from Bidarray the way crosses to the left bank via a small stone bridge soon after which the track to the left should be taken. After 3 km this leads finally to a small parking place. Continue on foot for some 2.5 km passing a farm with a large barn and 800m further when the track turns sharp left force your way straight ahead through the undergrowth to reach the river. The Put In is just downstream of an impassable stretch.

Take Out

This can be next to where the cars were initially left but an easier option is to carry on downstream some 300m towards the stone bridge over the now Bastan and rejoin the main track.

Description

After continuous rapids for a couple of kilometres the river settles down somewhat. The Class V sections are rather technical with narrows and ledges. Then the Bastan is no more than Class III (see below) and as mentioned above allows an easier Take out.

Le Bastan

4 km of Class III-III+   Kayaking ★ ★   Scenery ★ ★

The River

The Urrizate becomes the Bastan on flowing into France. A major left bank tributary joins at the border. Rainfall run off is again the main source of water and autumn and winter periods are the best times to ensure adequate water. The Bastan joins the Nive at **Biddarray.**

Put In

As described above for the take out for Urrizate.

Take Out

After the first stone bridge on the way up the valley - follow the track around 200 m downstream for access to the Take out.

Description

The run is without vices and provides good paddling.

Nive des Aldudes

8 km of Class II-III (4) D   Kayaking ★   Scenery ★★

The River

The Nive des Aldudes is a small rain-fed river that joins the Grande Nive just upstream of the village of **Osses** near the D 918. As with the Bastan paddling may only be viable in autumn and winter.

Put In

Follow the D 948 towards Banca and park near the hydro electric plant at the entrance to the village.

Take Out

The take out is just upstream of the village of **St. Etienne de Baigorry.**

Description

Set in the lovely Basque Hills the only proviso is the level of water. The Class 4 stretch involves technical passage between some large rocks.

Nive d'Estérençuby

9 km of Class III-IV   Kayaking ★   Scenery ★★

The River

This is another river that is dependant on rainfall for adequate water level.

Put In

From **St. Jean-Pied-de-Port** take the D 301 through **St. Michel** and **Estérençuby** and park at the road bridge near the isolated Hotel/Restaurant 'des Sources des Nives'. Total distance around 9km.

Take out

Cars can be left near the stone bridge just after **St. Michel.**

Description

The first 6 km to downstream of Estérençuby are Class III but look out for fallen trees. The 2 km of Class IV which follows contain a gorge stretch which can be observed from the road above.

BASSIN DU SAISON

N

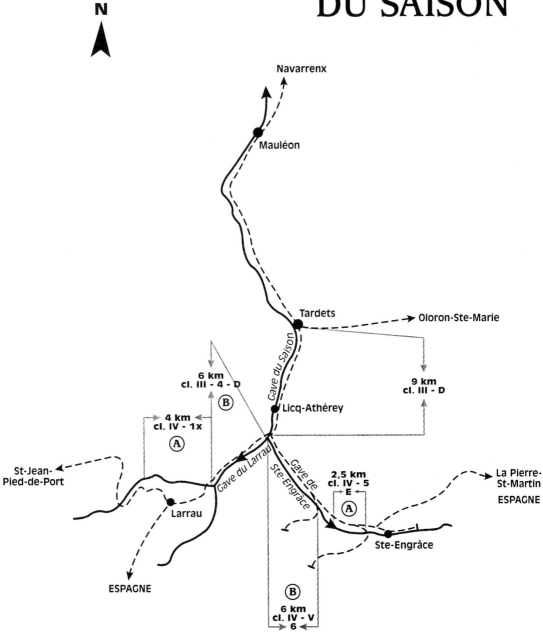

Navarrenx

Mauléon

Tardets → Oloron-Ste-Marie

Gave du Saison

6 km
cl. III - 4 - D
B

9 km
cl. III - D

4 km
cl. IV - 1x
A

Licq-Athérey

St-Jean-
Pied-de-Port

Gave du Larrau

Gave de Ste-Engrâce

2,5 km
cl. IV - 5
E
A

La Pierre-
St-Martin

ESPAGNE

Larrau

Ste-Engrâce

ESPAGNE

B
6 km
cl. IV - V
6

Bassin du Saison

Tourist Offices

Rafting & Kayak Companies

None advised.

ARAMITS (64570)
OFFICE DE TOURISME
Tél : 05.59.34.12.46

LA-PIERRE-ST-MARTIN (64570)
OFFICE DE TOURISME
Tél : 05.59.66.20.09, fax : 05.59.66.21.48

MAULEON-LICHARRE
OFFICE DE TOURISME
10, rue J.B. Heugas
Tél: 05.59.28.02.37, Fax: 05.59.28.02.21

TARDETS-SORHOLUS (64470)
OFFICE DE TOURISME
Place Centrale
Tél : 05.59.28.50.63, Fax : 05.59.28.52.46

Gave du Saison

9 km of Class III D   Kayaking ★★   Scenery ★

The River
The Gave du Saison begins at the confluence of the Gave du Larrau and Gave de Ste. Engrace. The latter brings a more stable supply of water and the although best outside dry summer months the Saison can normally be paddled **all year round**.

Put In
From the direction of Licq-Atherey follow the D 26 towards **Larrau**. After the junction with the D 113 the road crosses the river after about 200m. The put in is at the hydro-electric station near the bridge where the water from the Ste. Engrace and Larrau are re-introduced.

Take Out
In the village of **Tardets-Sorholus** take the left turn from the D 918 to shortly rejoin the Saison.

Description
The river provides a pleasant paddle without undue difficulty. The largest rapids are at the slalom course about 1 km from the start and can be portaged if necessary via the left bank.

At **Licq** it is best to portage the **weir** by stopping at the right bank about 50 m before the road bridge and level with the concrete steps to rejoin the river 200 m below.

Gave de Larrau "Parcours A".

Gave de Larrau

The River

Section A of the Gave de Larrau relies mainly on rainwater but the Gave d'Holcarte joining at Laugibar carries considerable water from snow melt. Unfortunately 2 km below here a barrage extracts water and thwarts good paddling for the remaining 4 km except in times of flood.

SECTION A

4 km of Class IV (x)   Kayaking ★★   Scenery ★★★

Put In

Leave **Larrau** via the D 19 in the direction of d'Iraty . The road rejoins the river after some 1.7 km at the Put In.

Take Out

This is 2.5 km downstream of Larrau at the Auberge de Logibar near the bridge on the D 26.

Description

The first 4 km of the descent is through woods and fallen trees may be encountered. The river is never wide and there are some narrow and technical passages.

There is an impossible bit about half way down caused by a partially blocked **siphon** which is best portaged via the field on the left bank before the footbridge.

For the record

We have also done a descent of the tributary joining the Larrau from the right near the Auberge de Logibar. This stream is very hemmed in and of no particular note apart from the setting. There are considerable portages necessary in two sections.

SECTION B - 'Classic'

6 km of Class III (4) D   Kayaking ★★   Scenery ★★★

Put In

At the Auberge de Logibar mentioned above.

Take Out

This is at the hydro-electric station at the confluence of the Gave Larrau and Gave Ste. Engrace 2km upstream of Licq Atherey on the D 26 towards Larrau.

Description

The D 26 follows the river throughout this section.

The barrage at Etchelu can be bypassed via the shoot on the right if water levels permit but further passage is only possible when enough excess water flows over the barrage. The water from the barrage is piped to the hydro-electric station at the Take Out described above.

Gave de Ste. Engrace (or Uhaitxa)

The River

The water of the Gave de Ste. Engrace is supplemented from neighbouring catchment areas but the barrage at the Gorge of Kakouetta limits paddling below to times of snow melt (April-May) or heavy rain. Section A can only be paddled after heavy rain.

SECTION A

2.5 km of Class IV (5) E   Kayaking ★★   Scenery ★★★

Put In

From the D26 take the D113 towards Ste Engrace and about 1.5 km after the signed path to the '**Gorges de Kakouetta**' turn off right to the nearby road bridge where you can put in.

Take Out

At the lake just downstream from the junction with the Kakouetta. Leave a car in the parking place for access to the gorges.

Description

At the put in the river is narrow but flow is soon supplemented by a tributary entering from the right. This marks the start of a more difficult stretch due to successions of ledges and drops. The river becomes gradually more powerful and enters a committing canyon where any egress is difficult. In this section there is a large angled ledge to avoid.

The end of the gorge is marked by what can at times be a jet of water between the rock faces which block the way. The left side is probably the best route through.

Take care to avoid **trees** which may block passage.

SECTION B ('Classic')

Class IV-V (6)   Kayaking ★★★   Scenery ★★

Put In

This is downstream of the Kakouetta Lake just before La Caserne on the D113 at the road bridge.

Take Out

From the D113 take the D 26 towards Larrau. The Take Out is at the nearby hydro-electric station at the confluence of the Gave Larrau and Gave Ste. Engrace.

Description

This is a magnificent run passing between huge rocks!

The Class 6 rapids are sometimes run but only at the right water levels - not too much, not too little. The first rapid is heralded by large old pillars at the edge of the river. Take out on the right bank to scout and portage.

The second Class 6 rapid is marked by an abrupt increase in the gradient of the river. At low water you may be able to stop on the flat rock in the middle and carry along the left hand side. In high water make sure you stop in good time on the **right** to portage.

The last 2 km are a mellow Class II-III.

Bassin du Gave d'Oloron

Tourist Offices

www.tourisme64.com

ARUDY (64260)
SYNDICAT D'INITIATIVE
Place de la Mairie
Tél : 05.59.05.77.11, Fax : 05.59.05.80.31

ACCOUS - VALLEE D'ASPE (64490)
OFFICE DE TOURISME
Moulin Bladé - RN 134
64490 BEDOUS

LARUNS (64440)
OFFICE DE TOURISME
Maison de la Vallée d'Ossau
Tél : 05.59.05.31.41, Fax : 05.59.05.35.49

NAVARRENX (64190)
OFFICE DE TOURISME
Porte St-Antoine
Tél : 05.59.66.10.22 (out of season),
05.59.66.14.93 (July and August)

OLORON-SAINTE-MARIE (64400)
OFFICE DE TOURISME
Tél : 05.59.39.98.00, Fax : 05.59.39.43.97

SAUVETERRE-DE-BEARN (64390)
SYNDICAT D'INITIATIVE
Place Royale
Tél : 05.59.38.58.65

Rafting & Kayak Companies

Centro Nautique de Soeix
64400 Oloron Ste Marie
Tel : 05 59 39 61 00, Fax :05 59 39 65 16

CPL Sports Place Camps
64260 Louvie-Juxon
Arudy
Tel: 05 59 05 82 28

Cup Pyrenees Eaux Vives
2 Av du Corps Franc Pommies
64110 Jurancon
Tel : 05 59 06 52 49, Fax : 05 59 06 46 72

Ossau Passion
Avenue Castellane
64440 Eaux-Bonnes
Tel : 05 59 05 43 14

Rafting Eaux-Vives
Le Pont
64190 Navarrenx
Tel : 05 59 66 04 05, Fax : 05 59 66 01 78

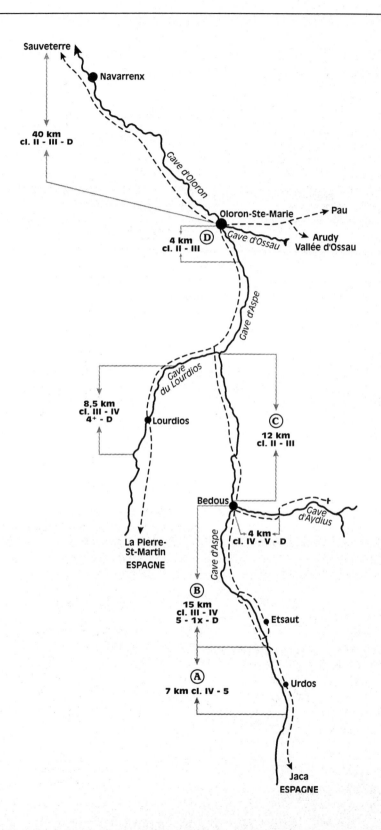

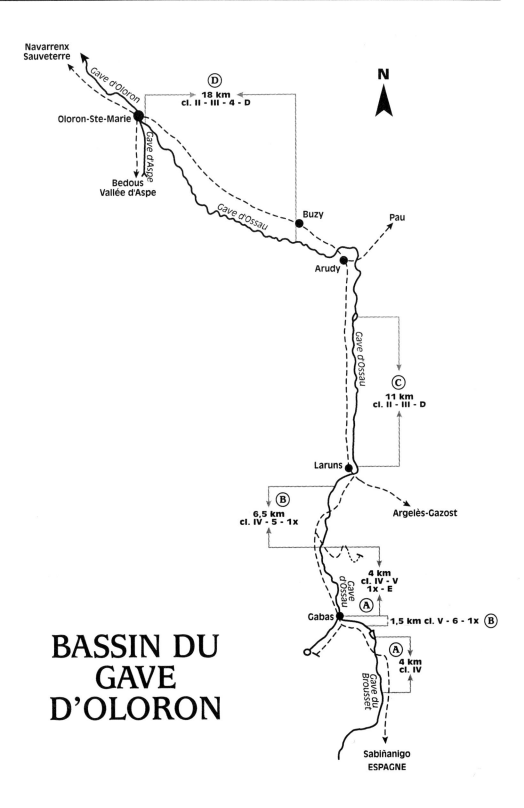

BASSIN DU GAVE D'OLORON

Gave d'Oloron

40 km of Class II-III D   Kayaking ★★   Scenery ★★

The River
The Gave d'Oloron begins at Oloron-Ste.-Marie at the confluence of the Gave d'Aspe and Gave d'Ossau. Fed by snow and rainfall the river can normally be paddled **all year round**.

Put In
This is in **Oloron-Ste.-Marie** on the left bank of the Aspe just above the confluence.

Take Out
In the village of **Sauveterre-de-Bearn**.   Both Oloron-Ste.-Marie and Sauveterre-de-Bearn lie astride the D936.

Description
You can break up this section as you wish - the road D 936 is never far away and allows access to a variety of villages en route.

The first half to **Navarrenx** has several artificial weirs which can be shot at low water levels or portaged - but take care to avoid the water inlets at these! The remaining section is very pretty and interesting enough despite some flat sections. Above **Sauveterre-de-Bearn** there are some Class II and occasionally some short Class III sections.

Gave d'Aspe "Parcours B".

Gave d'Aspe

The River

The Gave d'Aspe arises in Spain near the mountain (2570 m) of the same name and flows into France to join the Gave d'Ossau at Oloron and then becomes the Gave d'Oloran.

Fed by snow and rainfall the flow of the Aspe is interupted by numerous barrages but in May and after heavy rain can make a delightful paddle.

SECTION A

7 km of Class IV (5) Kayaking ★★   Scenery ★★

Put in

From Oloron go up the valley of the Aspe via the N134. Five kilometres after the village of **Urdos** there is a lake section of the river below which you can reach the river via a sloping field.

Take Out

This is level with the **Fort du Portalet** just below Urdos.

Description

This is best paddled using a short kayak - the first 2 km are narrow and have two Class 5. Note that the river bed may shift considerably in times of flood. The remainder of the run is more straight-forward but at high water the flow is rapid, eddies are scarce. Trees are a definite hazard.

SECTION B (from Fort du Portalet to Bedous)

15 km of Class III-IV (5) (x) D Kayaking ★★★ Scenery ★★★

Put In

As the take out for Section I above.

Take Out

At the campsite at **Bedous** on the left bank of the river on the road towards Lees-Athas and Osse en Aspe.

Description

The most difficult bit lies within the first 300 m just below the fort. This stretch can be avoided by putting in at the road bridge towards the village of Etsaut.

Watch out for the water extraction point 400m upstream of the road junction leading off the N 134 towards Lescun and 600m downstream **of La Goutte d'Eau**. Portage can be made around this on either bank.

After the village of **Cette-Eygun** the run becomes Class III to IV depending on water level.

SECTION C (from Bedous to Asasp)

12 km of Class II-III Kayaking ★★   Scenery ★★

Put In

Parking is possible on the level ground near the river just before the road climbs into nearby **Bedous**. The campsite at Bedous could also be used but a barrage has to be portaged almost immediately using the right bank.

Take Out

At the approach to the hydro-electric station 1 km above the village of **Asasp**. This is also the confluence with the Gave du Lourdios.

Description

This section is straightforward with the more major rapids near **Sarrance** and again about 400 m above the take out point. The latter can be examined from the road.

Taking into account the barrages - sufficient water is most likely from May till early June as the snow melts.

SECTION D (Soeix to Oloron)

4 km of Class II-III   Kayaking ★★   Scenery ★★

Put In

Take the N134 from Oloran-Ste-Marie towards the Spanish border and at the edge of town take the road to the left 100 m after the first roundabout. This leads to a building development but a right and a left turn will take you to the river just opposite the hydro-electric station of **Soeix**.

Take Out

Take out is in **Oloron** juste opposite the police station (Commissariat). If approaching Oloron from the direction of Pau then follow the signs to Saragosse and after the town centre and the public gardens the river will be on your left. The police station is opposite and parking is available in the adjacent area.

Take out from the river on the left bank just upstream of the 4m dam. Beware of the water outlet which is also on the left.

If you wish to continue down river then portage this dam via the right bank and a second one via the left bank to arrive at the confluence with the Gave d'Aspe and Gave d'Ossau which together now form the Oloran.

Description

This run is mostly interesting and pretty with the town area perhaps a little less so - rather spoilt by the engineering works for the town water supply.

Paddling is possible **all year round**.

Gave de Lourdios

8.5 km of class III-IV (4+) D   Kayaking ★ ★   Scenery ★

The River

The Gave de Lourdois is fed mainly by re-emergent underground water in the forest of Issaux arising from the eastern section of the limestone mass of Pierre St Martin. Paddling is possible when the thaw starts, from the beginning of April up until mid-May, as well as during periods of rainfall.

Put in

Go through the village of **Lourdios** and turn right after the road bridge in the direction of Pierre-St-Martin and Spain. Carry on for about 1.6 km until you reach a green gateway with a notice marked 'propriete privee'. The put in is below this small road at the level of the water release.

Take out

In the village of **Issor** where the road comes down close to the river.

Description

Almost as soon as you put in you find yourself in the midst of some pretty gorges. In the village of **Lourdios**, before putting on the water you can make out a small weir just downstream of the road bridge. After that, the road follows the river for almost all of this section.

After some technical descents visible from the road the river becomes quieter for or about 1 km before the sudden appearance of a class 4+ to 5 rapid, just after a small bridge surrounded by fields. The run then continues to the village of Issor and the confluence with the Gave d'Aspe, a 3 km stretch of Class II.

Gave d'Aydius

4 km of class IV-V D   Kayaking ★ ★   Scenery ★

The River

The mountain peaks of the water catchment area of the Gave d'Aydius rise to something in the region of 1900m. The thaw period is fairly short, from mid-April to mid-May but this river can also be paddled when rainfall is sufficient.

Put in

In the village of Bedous take the road towards the village of **Aydius** on the D 237. Carry on for 4 km until you reach the road bridge and the access point.

Take out

In **Bedous** village, immediately after the road bridge on the N 134 crossing the Aydius, take the road on the right towards the village of **Lees-Athas**. The take out is by the road bridge at the confluence of the Aydius and the Aspe.

Description

This descent is sustained and technical. You are advised to scout the sections before paddling them because of the possibility of fallen trees - the road follows the river along its length. Watch out for the **weir** just upstream of Bedous village which can be a keeper at high water levels.

Our scale for water flows:
- around 2 cumecs - ok;
- around 3 cumecs - entertaining,
- over 3 cumecs - serious.

For the record

We paddled above Aydius village – but this section is clogged with numerous tree-trunks.

Gave du Brousset "Parcours A".

Gave du Brousset

The river

The Brousset rises in the high valley of Ossau, in the region of the Aneou plateau, beneath mountain summits reaching more than 2300 m. It is fed by rain and melt water and water is not extracted from the first section so that it can be paddled from the first warmth at the end of April to the end of May and indeed up to the end of June following a snowy Winter. At Gabas it joins the Gave de Bious to form the Gave d'Ossau which itself joins the Gave d'Aspe at Oloron to form the Gave d'Oloron.

Water level:

There is a small house with a water gauge in the gorge 200 m upstream of the road bridge on the D 934 below a telephone booth. 50 cm is a recommended minimum, 120 cm maximum for paddling all the rapids.

SECTION A

4 km of class IV   Kayaking ★★★   Scenery ★★★

Put in

At a place called **'Caillou de Soques'** 4 km above the lake Fabreges on the D 934 the road takes an abrupt turn to the left. Parking is possible on both sides of the road and the river is reached across fields. The put in is near a small bridge.

Take out

At the lake of Fabreges.

Description

The first bit of the run passes through green fields and the occasional hazards are very visible. Then the river becomes canyon-like and the rapids more continuous. However, the road is never very far from the river, allowing scouting of all the rapids.

SECTION B

1.5 km of class V (6) (x)   Kayaking ★★   Scenery ★★

Note

In contrast to the previous section this one **rarely has enough water** because levels are affected by the lake at Fabreges and the hydroelectric installation at Artouste just upstream. You can chance it, however, during the thaw period from mid-May to the beginning of June.

Put in

There is a hydro-electric station (Artouste) about 2 km above Gabas on the D 934 in the direction of Spain. The put in is just downstream by a little bridge carrying the GR 10.

Take out

At the village of Gabas on the confluence of the Brousset and the Bious.

Description

This run is extremely attractive and the rapids very technical. The class 6 passage is a big slide of some 30m, quite paddleable at low water levels, just after the portage. You don't need lots of water to do this section, about 3 to 4 cumecs should be ok.

Gave du Brousset "Parcours A".

Gave d'Ossau

The River

The river starts at Gabas where the Brousset and the Bious join. Water levels fluctuate widely due to the presence of numerous dams. Sections A and B can be paddled during the thaw from May to the beginning of June.

SECTION A

4 km of class IV-V (x) E   Kayaking ★★★   Scenery ★★★

Put in

Downstream of the village of **Gabas** at the confluence of the Bious and the Brousset

Take out

2 km upstream of the hydro-electric station of **Miegebat** take the narrow road for the small valley of **Soussoueou**. After 800 m you can leave your car at the road bridge.

Description

This is a committing paddle with continuous rapids. The setting is superb, nestling in magnificent granite gorges.

A large **siphon** is followed by a chaos of rocks which is carried first on the left bank, then on the right. If the water level is very high it is impossible to put in again at the end of the chaos and you must make a long portage along the right bank - in which case it may be better to take out at this point as the following rapids could prove dangerous at high levels.

The best flow for this section is 4 to 6 cumecs.

SECTION B

6.5 km of class IV (5) (x)   Kayaking ★★★   Scenery ★★★

Put in

The put in for this section is where you take out for the previous one, at the road bridge on the road to the small valley of Soussoueou, 2 km upstream of the hydro-electric station at **Miegebat**.

Take out

Leaving Laruns in the direction of Spain towards the Gorges de Hourat, after 1.8 km a small bridge on the right with a large 'no entry' sign allows you into a parking area where you can leave your car.

Take out from the river on the right bank before the gorge closes in - the road and parking place are about 600 m away. If you miss the take out (best not to!) you can still take out in emergency a little further down on the left bank in a large eddy and carry back to the small bridge.

Description

This is a very attractive run and less testing than the previous one. The portage is 300 m below the **Miegebat hydro-electric station** on the left bank. You may wish to put in again directly below it. Once again you are paddling in beautiful granite gorges between huge rocks and with lovely rapids.

For the record

We have attempted the descent down as far as Laruns. It may be feasible at low water flows (1 to 2 cumecs) and by taking the appropriate ropes to climb down the dozen or so metres of the two waterfalls. This is probably of more interest to well-equipped canyoners than for kayakers!

SECTION C (Laruns to Castet)

11 km of class II-III D   Kayaking ★★   Scenery ★★

Put in

At the village of **Laruns** in the Pons area at the confluence of the Valentin and the Ossau.

Take out

On Castet lake in the village of **Castet** on the right bank of the Ossau.

Description

This is a section without too many difficulties but be wary of the trees that line the banks. Two-thirds down the descent is the **Barrage de Merville** which can be portaged on the left bank as the water extraction point is on the right.

You may find low water levels for the first few kilometres as the largest water release is at Geteu, 2 km downstream from Laruns, alongside the road - in which case you can put in at the hydro-electric station here.

You should find sufficient water along the whole of this section during the thaw period from mid-May to the beginning of June. From Geteu down you can usually paddle from the month of April up **until July** as long as there has been reasonable rainfall.

SECTION D (Buzy to Oloron)

18 km of class II-III (4) D   Kayaking ★★★   Scenery ★★★

Put in

In the village of **Buzy** arriving from Arudy take the left turn through the village and turn right to go down towards the motorcycle stadium and the hydro-electric station. The put in is at the station.

Take out

Going into **Oloron** from the Pau road turn left at the roundabout and drive for 150 m before you cross the Ossau then take a small road to the left, go through the entrance and leave your car in the car park on the left.

Description

This is a lovely run passing through the depths of an enchanting forest. The Class 4 rapid, called the 'Moulin Brule', is immediately after a small foot bridge. You can scout it by landing on the island.

After a long flat stretch there is a **dam** which can be shot using a slide on the left hand side. A bit further along, at the start of Oloron, there is another **dam** which can be shot depending on water levels. At higher levels this is better portaged on the left.

Bassin du Gave de Pau

Tourist Offices

ARGELES-GAZOST (65400)
OFFICE DE TOURISME
BP 35 - 65400 ARGELES-GAZOST
Tél : 05.62.97.00.25, Fax : 05.62.97.50.60

CAUTERETS (65110)
OFFICE DE TOURISME
Espaces-Cauterets
Place Foch - BP 79
65116 CAUTERETS Cedex
Tél : 05.62.92.50.27, Fax : 05.62.92.59.12

GAVARNIE- GÈDRE (65120)
(UNESCO World Heritage Site)
OFFICE DE TOURISME
65120 GAVARNIE
Tél : 05.62.92.49.10, Fax : 05.62.92.46.12

LOURDES (65100)
OFFICE DE TOURISME
Place Peyramale
65100 LOURDES
Tél : 05.62.42.77.40, Fax : 05.62.94.60.95,

PAU (64000)
OFFICE DE TOURISME
Place Royale (Hôtel de Ville)
Tél : 05.59.27.27.08, Fax : 05.59.27.03.21

PIERREFITTE-NESTALAS (65260)
OFFICE DE TOURISME
Avenue Jean Moulin
Tél : 05.62.92.71.31, fax : 05.62.92.71.31

LUZ-SAINT-SAUVEUR ((65120)
OFFICE DE TOURISME
Tél : 05.62.92.81.60, Fax : 05.62.92.87.19

Rafting & Kayak Companies

Relais d'Isaby (also Gite Auberge)
65460 Villelongue
ARGELES-GAZOST
Tel : 05 62 92 20 77, Fax: 05 62 92 22 01

Traquers de Vagues
Pont des Grottes de Betharram
LOURDES
Tel: 05 62 42 06 06

Ecolorado (also Gite Auberge)
65400 Agos
Lourdes
Tel : 05 62 97 54 54, Fax: 05 62 97 53 54

Adrenaline
65410 Sarrancolin
Tel : 05 62 98 73 25, Fax : 05 62 98 73 25

Pavilion des Sensations
10 des Arraildes
65400 Agos Vidalos
Tel : 05 62 97 05 90, Fax: 05 62 94 95 50

Aneto
Route de la Mongie
65710 Beaudean
Tel : 05 62 91 71 15, Fax : 05 62 91 74 98

Loisirs Aventures
65170 Cadelhan Torchere
Tel : 05 62 39 44 79

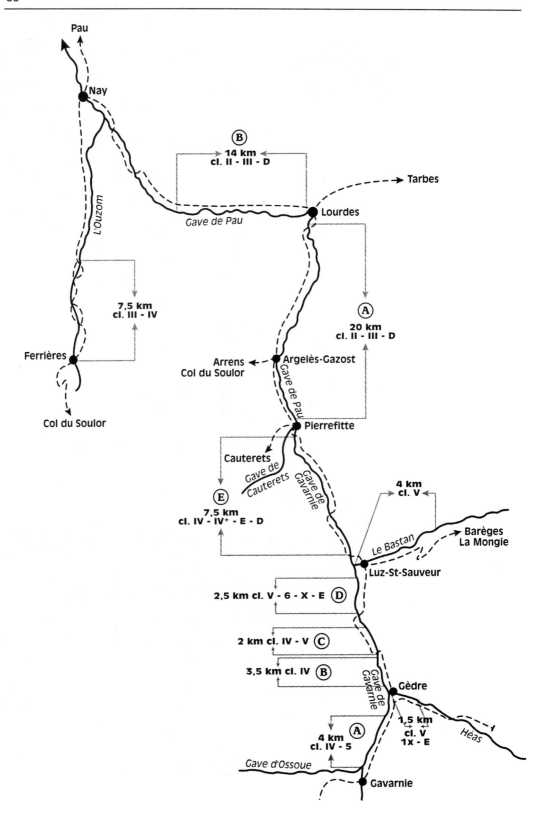

BASSIN
DU GAVE DE PAU

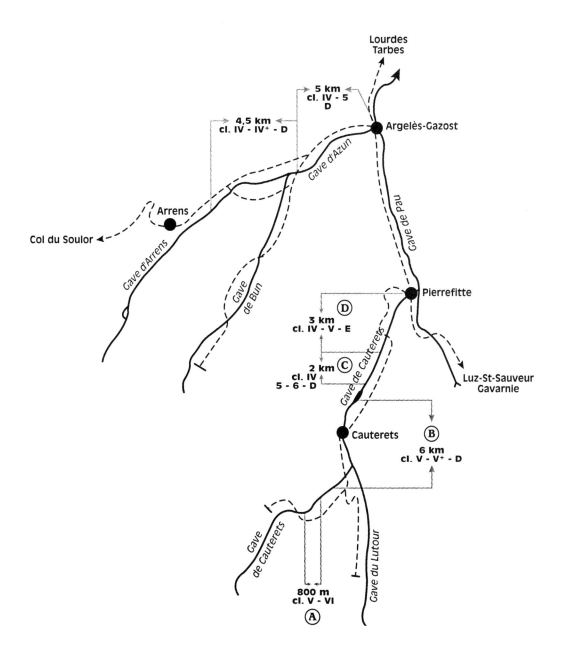

Gave de Pau

The River

The Gave du Pau arises from the confluence of the Gave de Cauterets and the Gave de Gavarnie at the village of **Pierrefitte**. Here the hydro-electric station feeds back in the water taken from the Bassins de Cauteret, Gavarnie and Bastin. This means that the Gave du Pau can be paddled **all year round.**

SECTION A (Pierrefitte to Lourdes)

20 km of Class II-III D   Kayaking ★★   Scenery ★

Put In

To get to the right river bank take the D 921 a short distance towards Luz St Saveur but almost immediately after crossing the river turn left onto the D13 to put in below the hydro-electric station.

Take Out

Just upstream of the city of **Lourdes** further along the N 21.

Description

The river bed is large and the clearly visible weirs can be shot or portaged. The flow is more sustained for the first 3 km.

SECTION B (Lourdes to Grottes de Betharram)

14 km of Class II-III D   Kayaking ★★   Scenery ★★

Put In

At the edge of Lourdes in the direction of St Pe de Bigorre. Take the minor left turn in the direction of the villages of Segus and Ossen to access at the nearby river bridge.

Take Out

This is at the **Grottes de Betharram** some 3 km downstream of St. Pe de Bigorre.

Description

The river is wide and weirs have slides for kayaks except the third weir at St. Pe de Bigorre, however this can usually safely be shot - but avoid the water pipe to the left. Take out at the slalom course at the Pont des Grottes de Betharram.

L'Ouzom

7.5 km of Class III-IV   Kayaking ★★   Scenery ★★

The River
This is a small river and the catchment is limited with a main thaw around mid May. Water is only likely to be adequate after heavy rain.

Put In
Near the Place d'Eglise in the village of **Ferrieres**

Take Out
It is preferable to take out about 3 km upstream of Arthez d'Asson where the road first splits.

Description
The river is narrow but the bed is well formed and gentle in gradient. The Class IV water is within the first third of the section. The road is never far from the river.

For the Record
We have paddled the section starting 3 km above Ferrieres from just above Arbeost. Numerous portages are necessary due to land slips into the river and the trip is not recommended.

Gave d'Arrens

4.5 km of Class IV-IV+   D   Kayaking ★★   Scenery ★★

The River
Because of the numerous barrages this river is only viable during water releases in dry periods in mid May to mid June or after very heavy rain.

Put In
At the village of **Argeles-Gazost** take the D 918 towards Arrens and the Col du Soulor. Just before **Aucun** take the narrow road to the left which leads immediately to a road bridge where river access is made.

Take Out
Upstream of Argeles take the left turn from the D 918 at **Arras** en Lavedan along the D 103 towards the lake of Estaing. The Take out is at about 2 km from Arras at the road bridge near the hydro-electric station.

Description
During the first 1 km the run is straight-forward but after the road bridge of the D 13 the gradient of the river increases markedly and in high water it does not appear safe to proceed, however at lower levels one can inspect the rapids first. The weir at mid section can normally be shot but portages past fallen trees might be necessary.

   If coming by car from Argeles you can assess the water level at the take out but note that a tributary- the Gave de Bun does add somewhat to the flow at this point.

Gave d'Azun

5 km of Class IV (5) D   Kayaking ★★   Scenery ★★

The River

This river begins at the confluence of the Gave d'Arrens and Gave de Bun at the village of **Arras** en Lavedan. Paddling is restricted by lack of water - see 'Gave d'Arrens' above.

Put In

This is the same as the take out point described above for the Arrens.

Take Out

At the confluence of the Azun and Pau at **Argeles** near the road bridge over the Gave de Pau.

Description

The river gradient on this run is somewhat less than the Arrens. Some pretty gorges are encountered just before the Class 5 bit - lying upstream of a footbridge. From the hydro-elctric water outlet to the confluence the enhanced river has some nice play waves to provide practice.

It is advised that you first assess the water level on your way to the start. On the drive out of Argeles on the D 921 towards Pierrefittte take the small road on the right just after the road bridge over the Arrens to end up just upstream of the water outlet from the hydro-elctric station where you can inspect the level.

Gave de Cauterets "Parcours B".

Gave de Cauterets

The River

The Gave de Cauterets arises at the foot of the Pic de Vignemale (3298 m). Sections A and B have no water abstraction points and thus Section A, which needs little water, is viable at the start of the thaw in early May and from the end of July to mid October. Section B is viable from mid May to the end of July and after melting early snow in autumn.

Sections C and D have most of their water abstracted and are only viable after heavy thaw say in mid May to mid June.

Water levels can be conveniently assessed from the gauge between the road bridges at **Raillere** on the outskirts of Cauterets. This is indicated from the road side by a solar panel.

A level of 140 indicates that Section B is ok but sections C and D are not really viable. Also to gain an idea of Section D there is a ring in the rock on the left bank above the road bridge in Pierrefitte. If the water is to the ring then the level is good but higher than this say up to the coping will produce Class V to V+ and beyond!

SECTION A (upper)

800 m of Class V-VI   Kayaking ★★★   Scenery ★★

Put In

On the D 920 at 5.5 km towards the Pont d'Espagne from **Cauterets** take the track to the right about 200 m below the 'Chute du Cerisey' to arrive at the access point.

Take Out

800 m below the Put In the river is impassable. This is heralded by a shootable drop, with the Take Out some 200 m below.

Description

A staircase of fine rapids, a gradient of around 100 m/km, and a superb 9 m shoot makes this section an exciting prospect. Best paddled at lower water levels of say 2-5 cumecs.

Some of this run can be seen from the road.

For the Record

The higher section of the Gave de Cauterets (also called the Gave du Marcadau) offers 2.5 km of Class IV water interrupted by many impassable drops. Carrying is also necessary to get to the water. The take out is at the Pont d'Espagne.

SECTION B ('classic')

6 km of Class V-V+ D   Kayaking ★★★   Scenery ★★

Put In

On the D 920 3 km towards the Pont d'Espagne from Cauterets there is a Thermal Station and souvenir shops etc.. This run starts nearby at the **Grande Dalle de la Raillere** about 100m upstream of the road bridge and just before the rocky section.

Take Out

At the barrage about 3 km downstream from Cauterets.

Description

With a gradient averaging around 50 m/km this SECTION also has some marked rapids which should be taken on the right. Near to the village of Cauterets the run is made more difficult by some artificial changes in the river bed causing some large slides and a succession of weirs.

In high water (above 140 on the scale referred to above) the Class rises to V-VI but you can put in at Cauterets near the car park for the cable lift and paddle the last 3 km (Class IV-V) to the barrage.

Note importantly that the small weir below the parking place should be shot at the edges and with plenty of pace. The other weirs do not present the same problem.

SECTION C (middle gorges)

2 km of Class IV (5-6) D   Kayaking ★★   Scenery ★★

Put In

4 km downstream of Cauterets at the **Calypso** hydro-electric station and below the large and impassable rock ledge.

Take Out

At the hydro-electric station about 200 m upstream of the D 920 road bridge and some 3 km above Pierrefitte-Nestalas.

Description

At good water levels this paddle is technical and of sustained difficulty. Fortunately many points can be observed from the road but there is a constant threat of fallen trees.

The three Class 5 rapids are near to each other upstream of a pretty gorge which itself is visible from the road. You are strongly advised to reconnoitre this stretch before paddling to ensure a clear passage exists.

The Class 6 rapid is at the start of the above gorge but this ugly looking drop can be portaged via the right bank.

SECTION D (lower gorges)

3 km of Class IV-V E   Kayaking ★★★   Scenery ★★

Put In
This is at the previous take out.

Take Out
At **Pierrefitte-Nestalas** just downstream of the road bridge on the D 921.

Description
Although more enclosed than the previous section this is a good paddle at the right water levels. Beware of the first artificial change of slope above the road bridge in Pierrefitte.

Note
The absence of barrages, etc. on the higher sections means that even if there is insufficient water on sections C and D then there is still good prospects of paddling sections A and B If however, sections C and D are viable the river levels will most likely be too high for the upper sections.

Gave de Cauterets, "partie haute".

*Jeannot sur le gave
de Gavarnie
"parcours classique".*

La gorge de départ
du "parcours classique",
gave de Gavarnie.

Pierre et Kiki en action sur le Ste-Engrâce.

Gave du Bastan

4 km of Class V   Kayaking ★★★   Scenery ★★

The River

The Gave du Bastan has most water supplied from the Massif de Neouvielle which rises to 3000 m. The nearby Col Du Tourmalet is well known to cycling enthusiasts.

Much water is abstracted and the flow is thus subject to wide variation and paddling possibilities are thus restricted to times of rapid thaw at the end of May and beginning of June.

Put In

At **Luz-St-Sauveur** take the D 918 towards Bareges and after two hairpin bends at about 4 km, look out for the Put In at a small bridge on the left just before the hydro-electric station.

Take Out

Either take out at the village of Luz-St-Saveur or near the D 921 road bridge over the Gavarnie about 2 km downstream.

Description

This river demands a high level of expertise to cope with the gradient of 65 m/km and the danger posed by fallen trees. The best level is at 1 m on the gauge downstream right bank of the road bridge in Luz-St-Sauveur.

For the Record

Above Bareges up to the hydro-electric station the whole run is made difficult by debris in the river near Bareges.

Gave d'Héas.

Gave d'Heas

1.5 km of class V (x) E   Kayaking ★★   Scenery ★★★

The River
This is typical small river of the region, dependant on melt water and with limited valley slopes, paddling possibilities are limited to about 3 weeks a year around the beginning of June.

Put in
1 km after leaving the village of **Gèdre** turn to the left on the D 922 towards the amphitheatre at Troumouse and the Gloriettes lake. After another 1 km where there is a foot path to the right leading to the lake, take the track going down to the river.

Take out
Either at the restaurant 'la Cascade' in Gèdre on the left before the bridge, or at the confluence of the Heas and the Gavarnie, taking the road into Gèdre and just after the bridge to the right.

Description
This run is very canyon-like and technical with some lovely drops. It is advisable to try and scout as much as you can of the upper parts of the gorge before getting on the water. Given the narrowness of the river bed the water level should not be too high (we think about 2 cumecs). Although the run is short you need to allow about 3 to 4 hours.

After the portage on the left bank, there is a drop which you run blind (scouting is difficult perched on a cramped rock at the entry to the run). Take a right or left angle and not the main shoot where a rock is lurking in the middle.

For the record
We have paddled the 2 km upstream of the put in but it was a succession of portages - just hard work and little interest.

Gave de Gavarnie

The River
The Gavarnie is one of those Pyrenean rivers that is very important both from the point of view of sporting activities and also thanks to its sublime natural setting. This river has its source in the midst of mountain peaks of more than 3000 m and its classic section can be paddled from the beginning of the thaw.

Guidance on water levels
Due to the numerous barrages, normally when section E is feasible then you are sure to strong levels of water in the classic section, which has no dams. If there is a good level of water in the classic section, section B and, sometimes, section C can be paddled. As for section D - this is better paddled when there is very little water.

SECTION A ('classic')

4 km of class IV (5)   Kayaking ★★★   Scenery ★★★

Put in
Pass the village of **Gèdre** on the D 921 and climb in the direction of **Gavarnie**. Where there is the sign showing the entry to the village take the little road which goes down on the right towards the purification plant. Leave your car on this road and continue through fields to cross a small stone bridge and put in on the left bank just at the confluence of the Ossoue and the Gavarnie.

Take out
About 3.5 km above **Gèdre** you can pick out between the huge rocks lining the road the 'Chaos of Coumely'. Sure enough, the take out is upstream of the chaos!

Description
This magnificent run has alternating rock-strewn rapids and relaxed intervals. Don't forget to keep turning round to admire the rocky amphitheatre.

The drop below the bridge at the put in is left for your own judgement! The class 5 rapid is a large drop which you come to in the first half of the descent. The road follows the river for two-thirds of the run.

For the record
We did attempt to put in above the village of Gavarnie - a run peppered with siphons and not recommended.

SECTION B (Gèdre to Pragneres)

3.5 km of Class IV   Kayaking ★★★ Scenery ★★

Put In
Near Gèdre take the road towards the campsite and stop before the bridge to gain access to the river below the barrage.

Take Out
At the hydro-electric station near the D 921 at Pragneres.

Description
This is a pleasant paddle with well defined rapids but only normally viable during heavy thaws from late May to the beginning of June. There are some good beaches for rest and recuperation - some of which are visible from the road.

For the Record

We tried the section above this: There are numerous falls, two rocky rapids and portages are necessary. We don't recommend it but if you want to, it is best attempted at low water levels.

SECTION C (Pragneres to Sia)

2 km of Class IV-V

Kayaking ★★★ Scenery ★★

Put In

Below the hydro-electric station at Pragneres.

Take Out

5 km upstream of Luz-St-Sauveur level with **Sia** and above an impassable waterfall. From the river regain the road 200 m above the bridge via the left bank.

Description

More sustained flows than the previous sections and often very technical. Water is still however rarely adequate for paddling.

SECTION D (Gorges de Sia)

2.5 km of Class V (6) (xxx) E

Kayaking ★★★ Scenery ★★

Put In

This is at the hamlet of **Sia** on the D 921 between Luz-st-sauveur and Gavarnie. Go down to the left and cross the wood.

Take Out

Under the **Pont Napoleon** 2 km above Luz-St-Saveur towards Gavarnie on the D 921.

Description

This run is narrow and constrained by magnificent gorges. There are some beautiful shoots and several unrunnable drops where portages are necessary - particularly noteworthy is a double ledge which can only be portaged in low water. This is a committing run that should only be attempted in low water.

SECTION E (Gorges de Luz)

7.5 km of Class IV-IV+ E D

Kayaking ★★★ Scenery ★★★

Put In

At the road bridge on the D 921 and 1.5 km downstream of Luz-St-Sauveur.

Take Out

At the road bridge on the D 921 and 1.7 km upstream of **Pierrefitte-Nestalas.**

Description

The first part of the run up to the half way road bridge is Class III+ but the second is much more technical. Note that in high water any swim may be long due to the steep banks.

Half way up the valley it is best to scout the barrage and portage at the hydro-electric station below the bridge.

Gave d'Ossau "Parcours A".

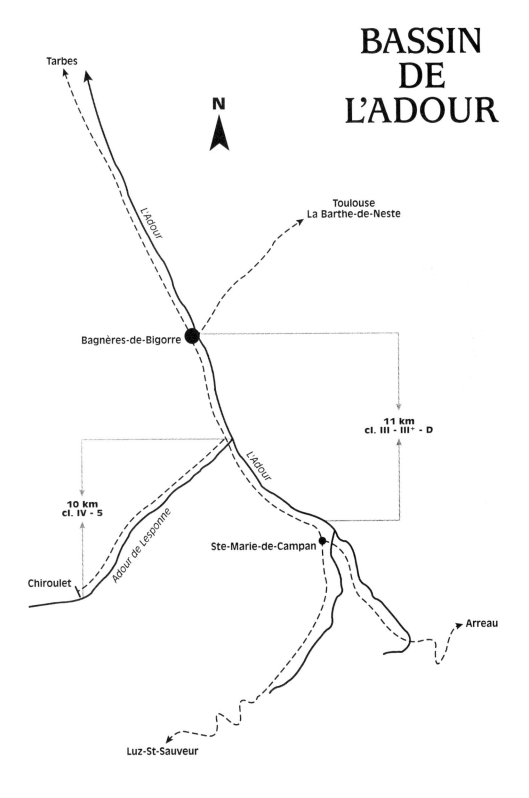

Tarbes

N

BASSIN DE L'ADOUR

L'Adour

Toulouse
La Barthe-de-Neste

Bagnères-de-Bigorre

11 km
cl. III - III$^+$ - D

L'Adour

10 km
cl. IV - 5

Adour de Lesponne

Ste-Marie-de-Campan

Chiroulet

Arreau

Luz-St-Sauveur

Bassin de l'Adour

Tourist Offices

www.hautebigorre.com

BAGNERES-DE-BIGORRE (65202)
OFFICE DE TOURISME
3, Allées Tournefort - BP 226
65 202 BAGNERES-DE-BIGORRE
Tél : 06.62.95.50.71, Fax : 05.62.95.33.13,

CAMPAN (65710)
OFFICE DE TOURISME
Tél : 05.62.91.70.36, Fax : 05.62.91.61.26

TARBES (65000)
3, Cours Gambetta
Tél : 05.62.51.30.31, Fax : 05.62.44.17.63

Rafting & Kayak Companies

Haut Pyrenees Sport Nature
Base de Loisirs - la Pradette
65270 St Pe de Bigorre
Tel : 05 62 41 81 48, Fax: 05 62 41 87 46

L'Adour

11 km of Class III-III+ D   Kayaking ★★   Scenery ★★

The River

Formed by the confluence of the Adour de Gripp and the Adour de Payolle, the Adour is fed by thaw and thus viable in May to early June. This period may be extended by heavy rain.

There is a water gauge on the way to the Centre de Vacances (CCAS) within the village of **Campan** on the D 935. The turn to the centre is to the left at 200 m up the valley from the village square. A reading of 25 on the scale indicates a minimum level for paddling.

A second gauge is found under the road bridge upstream of the slalom site at **Bagneres-de-Bigorre**. Here a reading above 65 indicates a satisfactory level for the stretch from Baudéan.

Put In

This is at 1 km above Ste-Marie-de-Campan near the cliffs.

Take Out

Within **Bagneres-de-Bigorre** take the D 938 road towards Capvern-les-Bains to soon join the river. Turn left just before the nearby road bridge to the Take Out at the base of the Slalom course.

Description

The first 6 km rarely have adequate water but things are much better after the confluence with the Adour de Lesponne at **Baudéan**. You can put in here at the hydro-electric station and enjoy the section of rapids on the slalom course at the Take Out.

L'Adour de Lesponne

10 km of Class IV (5)   Kayaking ★★★   Scenery ★★

The River

The Adour de Lesponne feeds into the Adour at **Baudéan**. This is a good paddle during a rapid thaw from April or after heavy rain.

Put In

At Beaudean take the D 29 to access the river at **Chiroulet**.

Take Out

This is at the road bridge just before the confluence with the Adour just above **Baudéan**.

Description

Set in lovely scenery the river is narrow and twisting and fallen trees may be encountered. At the halfway point a tributary enters from the left and provides an alternative Put In if water levels above are insufficient.

If desired the trip can be extended to Bagneres-de-Bigorre (see above).

La Neste d'Aure.

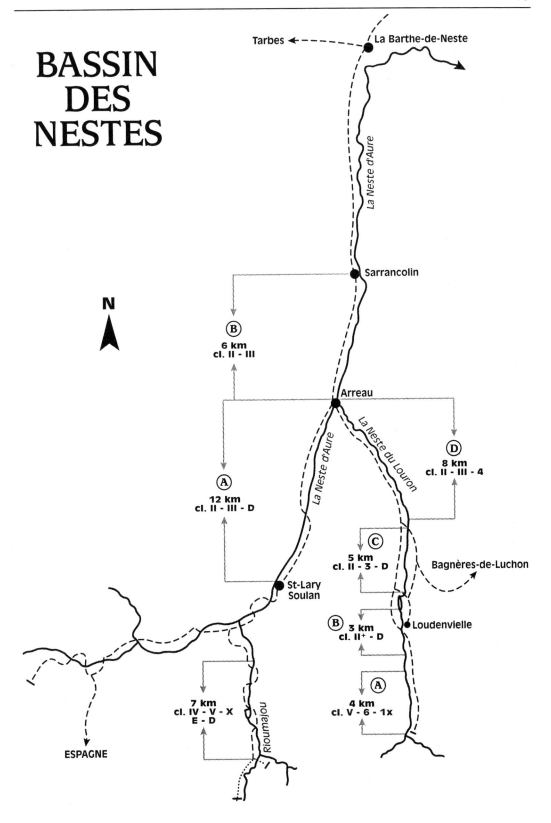

BASSIN
DES
NESTES

N

Tarbes ← La Barthe-de-Neste

La Neste d'Aure

Sarrancolin

Ⓑ
6 km
cl. II - III

Arreau

La Neste du Louron

La Neste d'Aure

Ⓓ
8 km
cl. II - III - 4

Ⓐ
12 km
cl. II - III - D

Ⓒ
5 km
cl. II - 3 - D

Bagnères-de-Luchon

St-Lary
Soulan

Ⓑ 3 km
cl. II⁺ - D

Loudenvielle

7 km
cl. IV - V - X
E - D

Rioumajou

Ⓐ
4 km
cl. V - 6 - 1x

ESPAGNE

Bassin des Nestes

Tourist Offices

LANNEMEZAN (65300)
OFFICE DE TOURISME
1, place de la République
Tél : 05.62.98.08.31, Fax : 05.62.40.21.50

SAINT-LARY-SOULAN (65170)
OFFICE DE TOURISME
37, rue Principale
Tél : 05.62.39.50.81, Fax : 05.62.39.50.06,

SARRANCOLIN (65410)
SYNDICAT D'INITIATIVE
Tél : 05.62.98.79.88

Rafting & Kayak Companies

Adrenaline
Saint Lary Soulan
Tel : 05 62 40 04 04

Neste d'Aure.

La Neste d'Aure

The River

This river has its source in the heart of the central Pyrenees and therefore definitely depends upon both rain and melt water. It can be paddled **all year** long for most of the sections described, however the best water levels are during the thaw from the beginning of May up to June, or at times of heavy rainfall.

SECTION A   (from St Lary to Arreau)

12 km of class II-III D   Kayaking ★ ★   Scenery ★ ★

Put In

In the village of **St Lary** at the 'Maison de l'Ours'.

Take out

The take out is at the downstream edge of the village of **Arreau** at the dam.

Description

From the village of St Lary to the road bridge 5 km downstream the river is class II-III flowing over gravel beds with no particular difficulty. This part is feasible during the thaw or in rainy periods. After the road bridge the degree of difficulty is about the same but a water release a bit further downstream allows paddling all year long as far as Arreau.

7 km lower down as you arrive at the village of Cadeac you will come across a **dam** which can be shot with no problem thanks to the kayak slide provided. Once through, don't forget to pull the lever to let down the trap door down again. The next stretch of river down to Arreau is a nice continuous class III.

For the record

We ran the river further upstream from a put in at the confluence of the Neste de Saux and the Neste de la Gela and took out at the town of Fabian. Because the river is hemmed in by steep sides we were not able to reach the hydro-electric station of Fabian. Vertical rock faces and a succession of rapids stopped us from achieving our aim and we had to leave the gorge using climbing ropes about 300m before the station. This section is committing with drops that are difficult and almost impossible to portage. (photos pages 74 & 76 were taken on this stretch.)

SECTION B (from Arreau to Sarrancolin)

6 km of class II-III   Kayaking ★ ★   Scenery ★

Put in

Downstream of the dam at **Arreau**.

Take out

At the dam at **Sarrancolin**

Description

This is a pleasant section with no special difficulty and the road is never far away. Unfortunately it can only be paddled when there is an overflow of water at the Arreau dam due to lots of melt water or after rainy periods.

Neste de Louron

The River

The Neste de Louron is a tributary of the Neste d'Aure. The very high mountain summits towering over this relatively hemmed in valley provide water which is ideal for white water activities. Unfortunately, as usual, the number of water extraction points works against us and limits times of paddling to when there is overflow from the dams, mainly during the thaw between mid-May and mid-June and after heavy rain.

SECTION A (from the bridge at Prat to the chaos)

4 km of class V (6) (x)   Kayaking ★★   Scenery ★★

Put In

To rach the put in drive along the valley of Louron to **Pt de Prat** and put in at the water inlet point.

Take out

The take out is about 4 km downstream of the put in, before the chaos, which is a characteristic feature visible from the road.

Description

The river course is narrow and technical, the rapids continuous and the river falls from drop to drop. However, the road is never far away.

Section B (from Thermes to the lake)

3 km of class II+ D   Kayaking ★★   Scenery ★★

Put In

For the put in, drive along the valley of Louran to the thermal baths, put in beneath the water extraction point 2 km upstream of the village of **Loudenvielle**.

Take Out

At the dam of lake Loudenville.

Description

The river has wooded banks and is not very big with pleasant paddling through small rapids. Upstream of the road bridge at Loudenvielle two small drops become stoppers at high water level. This section can be paddled for a good part of the year **including the Summer**.

SECTION C (from the lake at Loudenvielle to Avajan)

5 km of class II (3) D

Put In

This is about 100 m downstream from the lake at the water outlet point.

Take out

The take out is under the road bridge on the D 618 the main road between Arreau and the col de Peyresourde. There is a water inlet point a little downstream.

Description

This section is similar to the previous one with the river running over gravel beds in attractive undergrowth. Paddling can be done for **most of the Summer** season. The class 3 bit is a weir at a mill, which can be scouted from the take out road bridge.

SECTION D (from Avajan to Arreau)

8 km of class   II-III (4)   Kayaking ★★   Scenery ★★

Put In

Beneath the hydro-electric station downstream of the road bridge on the D 618.

Take Out

After the confluence with the Neste d'Aure, downstream of the village of **Areau** at the lake and before the dam.

Description

The river bed is narrow and this is a technical run. After slightly more than 1 km you come across the class 4 rapid - a large drop which can be scouted before putting on. The road runs fairly close to this section all the way up the valley. About 1 km upstream of Arreau the Neste de Louron recovers the water flow diverted at the put in point, so giving plenty of volume to finish the run.

Normally this run can only be paddled when there is plenty of thaw from mid-May to mid-June or after rainy periods.

Rioumajou

7 km of class IV-V (xxx) E D   Kayaking ★   Scenery ★ ★

The River

The Rioumajou is a tributary to the right of the Nest d'Aure. Its source is in peaks of between 2500 and 3000 m altitude but even so the thaw period is rather short, occurring during the course of May when it is very warm. Unfortunately there is also a large dam which diverts the water for most of the river.

Put In

About 3.5 km upstream of **St Lary** in the direction of Spain take the road towards the village of **Tramezaigues**. Go through the village and drive up the valley of Rioumajou to the barns at **Fredancon**. The put in is there, just before the confluence with a beautiful right bank tributary.

Take Out

The take out is about 200 m upstream of the water extraction point at **Maison Blanche** on the side of the road a few hundred metres upstream of the village of **Tramezaigues**.

Description

The first kilometre is easy, the river running over gravel beds before becoming constricted into very narrow passages which need to be scouted before you run them.

The portage at the lake is on the right bank. We advise you to carry for 700 m to a very large rock at the side of the road. You can put in here on the left bank using ropes. From here the descent is canyon-like for 1 km with one problem-free portage. Then the rock walls open up and you reach a small chaos, visible from the road, which must be portaged. From there to the take out the river is deeper and technical.

You may wish to scout the stretch of gorge before putting on. For all of the run, beware of trees which are close to the water.

There is a **water gauge** 500 m upstream of the dam where there are some solar panels at the side of the road. Probably 1.60 cumecs is a good flow for the section upstream of the lake and, if the volume of water diverted at the lake is constant, also good for the canyon stretch but slightly skimpy for the more open part after the chaos. Avoid putting on again just after the dam because there is a large hazard which cannot be carried and you will have to climb back out of the gorge.

Le Rioumajou.

Bassin de la Garonne

Tourist Offices

www.luchon.com
www.stgaudens.com

ASPET (31160)
OFFICE DE TOURISME
Tél : 05.61.94.86.51

BAGNERES-DE-LUCHON (31110)
OFFICE DE TOURISME
18, Allées d'Etigny - BP 29
Tél : 05.61.79.21.21, Fax : 05.61.79.11.23

MONTREJEAU (31210)
OFFICE DE TOURISME
Place Valentin Abeille
Tél : 05.6195.80.22

SAINT-BEAT (31440)
OFFICE DE TOURISME
Avenue de la Gerle
Tél : 05.61.79.45.98

SAINT-GAUDENS (31800)
OFFICE DE TOURISME
2, rue Thiers
Tél : 05.61.94.77.61, Fax : 05.61.94.77.50

Rafting & Kayak Companies

Antignac
Base d'eau vive
9 chemin du Poy
Tel : 05 61 79 19 20

Virgule 7
4 Place du Comminges
31110 Bagneres du Luchon
Tel : 05 61 79 01 97

Base d'eau vive
31110 Antignac
Tel : 05 61 79 19 20, Fax : 05 61 79 60 81

Aventure Raid Cie
Barbazon
Tel : 05 61 79 61 10

Les Pagaies
Valcabrere
Tel : 05 61 08 74 40

BASSIN DE LA GARONNE

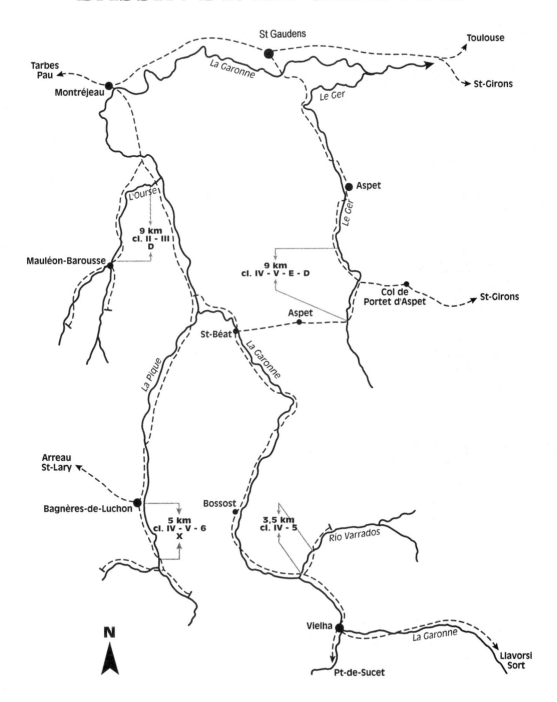

St Gaudens

Toulouse

Tarbes
Pau

La Garonne

St-Girons

Montréjeau

Le Ger

Aspet

L'Ourse

Le Ger

**9 km
cl. II - III
D**

**9 km
cl. IV - V - E - D**

Mauléon-Barousse

Col de
Portet d'Aspet

St-Girons

Aspet

St-Béat

La Garonne

La Pique

Arreau
St-Lary

Bagnères-de-Luchon

Bossost

**5 km
cl. IV - V - 6
X**

**3,5 km
cl. IV - 5**

Río Varrados

N

Vielha

La Garonne

Llavorsi
Sort

Pt-de-Sucet

L'Ourse

9 km of Class II-III D   Kayaking ★   Scenery ★

The River

The catchment extends only to medium altitude (1900-2100 m) and so the short thaw only gives good water in mid May. There may be a better chance of paddling after heavy rain. The river picks up the Ourse de Ferrere at Mauleon-Barousse to enter the Garonne from the left at Loures-Barousse.

Put In

Access is just upstream of **Mauleon-Barousse**.

Take Out

This is at **Izaourt** on the D 26 just off the N125 near Loures-Barousse.

Description

This narrow river flows through the Forest of Barousse and more open countryside. The gradient is a little more sustained early on and the small weirs are easily passable.

Le Ger

9 km of Class IV-V E D   Kayaking ★★★   Scenery ★★

The River

With a similar type of catchment and availability as the Ourse, the Ger joins the Garonne from the right at **Labarthe-Inard**.

Put In

At St. Gaudens take the D 5 road to Aspet and on to Henne-Morte. Here take the right turn (D 85) towards the Col de Mente and St Beat. The access is under the road bridge at the village of **Couledoux**.

Take Out

This is at the road bridge 4 km downstream of Henne-Morte and just upstream of **Razecueille**.

Description

Afer a succession of rapids for the first kilometres the river then calms down somewhat until a difficult section at the road bridge above **Henne-Morte**. This section should be scouted before attempting it - a dam and a succession of rapids in mid stream give a narrow passage and fallen trees make egress difficult.

   The trip can be extended for about 6 km at an easier Class II-III (4). Take out 1 km above Aspet where the road again crosses the river.

Rio Varrados

3.5 km of Class IV (5)   Kayaking ★★   Scenery ★★

The River
The Varrados is a right bank tributary of the river Garonne, quite far upstream. It is normally runnable from mid May to mid June and has a catchment extending to 2500m.

Put In
Take the N 230 south from France into Spain and take a left turn 6 km upstream of **Bossost** towards Vielha. This follows the Varrados (Barrados) from the Garonne to the access point near the road bridge found after some 3.5 km.

Take Out
At the confluence with the Garonne.

Description
This narrow river falls regularly and provides an agreeable paddle. Some sections are a bit more demanding and beware of fallen trees.

For the Record
The much steeper higher section appears to be viable- but should be left to the experts!

Río Varrados.

Bassin du Salat

Tourist Offices

AULUS-LES-BAINS (09200)
SYNDICAT D'INITIATIVE
Tél : 05.61.96.01.79

BIROS-SENTEIN (09800)
OFFICE DE TOURISME
09800 SENTEIN
tél : 05.61.96.10.90

CASTILLON-EN-COUSERANS (09800)
OFFICE DE TOURISME
Tél : 05.61.96.72.64

SAINT-GIRONS (09200)
OFFICE DE TOURISME
Place Alphonse Sentein
Tél : 05.61.96.26.60, Fax : 05.61.96.26.69

Rafting & Kayak Companies

Label Bleu
Base de Moulin
Seix
Tel : 05 61 66 89 31

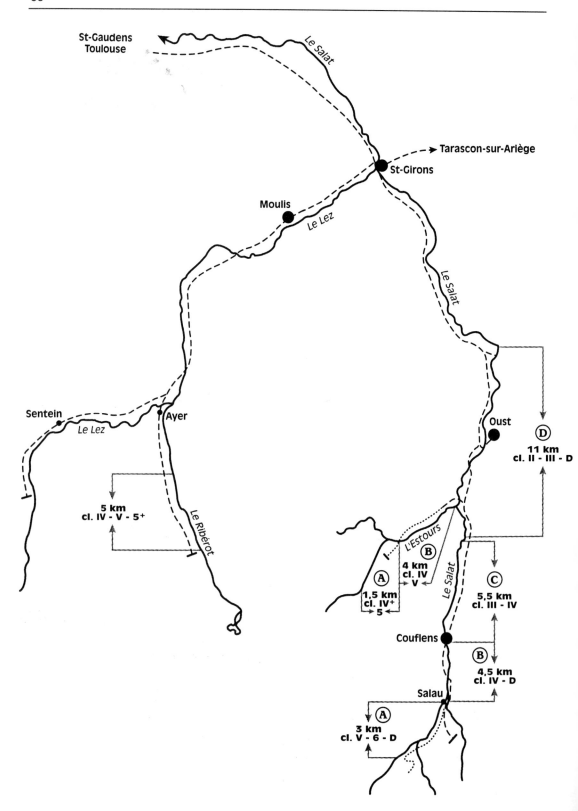

BASSIN
DU SALAT

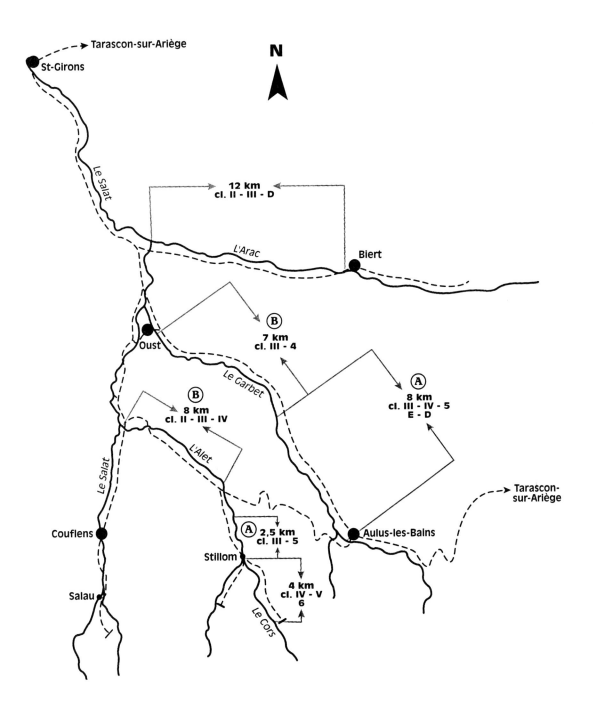

Le Riberot

5 km of Class IV-V (5+)   Kayaking ★★★   Scenery ★★

The River

The Riberot is a right bank tributary of the **Lez** which itself joins the Salat at **St. Girons**. The catchment relies on thaw from late May to mid June and may also be viable at other times after heavy rain.

Put In

From **St. Girons** go up the Lez valley on the D 618 and from Andressein on the D 4 to Les Bordes. A left turn at 2 km off the road towards Bonac takes you up the Riberot via the hamlet of **Ayer**. Follow the track to the end for the put in.

Take Out

This is 5 km downstream at the dam above Ayer.

Description

Rapid flow is sustained along the whole of the run. Technical rapids are found between large granite blocks.

In the middle of a narrow stretch a class 5+ drop can only be run in high water (but this is not advised). The approach to this fall is indicated by a footbridge about a 100 m upstream - portage on the left.

Le Salat

The River

The Salat has many tributaries including the Alet, Estours and Garbet. Except for the upper section where the water flow might be restricted, the remainder of the Salat should have good water for much of May and June.

The rivers of the Salat system are remarkable for the **potential and variety** that they offer the paddler.

SECTION A (upper)

3 km of Class V (6) D   Kayaking ★★★   Scenery ★★

Put In

Drive up the D 3 road from **Pont de la Taule** though Couflens and Salau. After Salau and a second hair pin bend a track continues straight ahead and access is gained from this at the confluence of two streams.

Take Out

At the village of **Sallau**.

Description

This run is only interesting in high water. The river is twisting, steep and technical. There is a class 6 stretch about 1 km downstream from the put in, near a barn and below an old foot bridge - this is worth inspecting before embarking.

A bit lower down a dam can normally be shot on the extreme right. Good technique is still required for the rest of the run.

SECTION B (from Salau to Couflens)

4.5 km of Class IV D Kayaking ★★ Scenery ★★

Put In

Drive up the valley of the Salat to access the river at the bridge in **Salau**.

Take Out

Under the road bridge leading to the cemetery in **Couflens**.

Description

A sustained and busy paddle for all its length - grab the chance for a run if the water level is sufficient.. At 100 m above the takeout a causeway can be shot on the right but beware at all water levels. The road follows the river throughout.

At Couflens there is jealously guarded fishing and an attempt may be made to stop your passage. However, they are not within their rights to do this!

SECTION C (from Couflens to Pont de la Taule)

5.5 km of Class III-IV Kayaking ★★ Scenery ★★

Put In

At the take out as above.

Take Out

This is made at the right bank just above the village of Pont de la Taule. A large parking area is available.

Description

This section is distinctly less steep than that above but never the less can provide good paddling. Beware of fallen trees.

The road follows the river throughout.

SECTION D (from Pont de la Taule to Kercabanac)

11 km of Class II-III D Kayaking ★ Scenery ★★

Put In

At the above take out

Take Out

An easy exit can be made on the left bank at **Kercabanac** where the Arac tributary enters.

Description

The Salat receives the water of the Alet and Estours in this section so levels are more sustained than earlier runs. Paddling is enjoyable and without any especial hazards with the first part of the run having a faster flow.

Just upstream of **Soueix** is a barrage which has a kayak slide to the right which should be used because of the dangerous stopper on the rest of the weir.

After this easy paddling continues to just above Lacourt where the take out is on the right bank at the barrage.

(Further downstream towards St. Girons is not recommended because of some dangerous dams).

L'Estours

The River

This tributary of the Salat receives adequate snow melt normally from a late May to early June thaw The barrage at the start of Section B takes much water and must be in a state of overflow for the river to be viable below.

SECTION A

1.5 km of Class IV+ (5)   Kayaking ★ ★ ★   Scenery ★ ★ ★

Put In

Driving up the valley above **Seix** on the D 3, after 3 km take the right turn at Moulin Lauga and after passing the hamlet of **Estours** proceed further up the track of the GR 10 to the barrage. A few hundred metres further and the track stops and kayaks must be carried. Follow the path to reach the river in about 5 minutes where a footbridge spans a gorge. You can choose to put in on the right above and shoot this magnificent gorge, or put in about 100m below the foot bridge on the left bank.

Take Out

At the barrage

Description

The river is narrow and rocky and gradient is sustained. The gorge section is very confined and committing - note that there is a drop at the end of the gorge that is not visible from the footbridge, but which can be inspected from the left bank.

For the record

We had the idea of doing the higher section and there are two possibilities:
1. Continue carrying along the path upstream and inspecting as you go.
2. Organise a shuttle via Couflens and the Col de Pause. From there a path leads to the
    sources of the Estours. Note the errors here in the IGN map no 2048.

We advise against any attempt when the barrage is discharging. The scenery is magnificent with the background of a snow covered Mount Valio, whilst the river is steep and challenging with numerous fallen trees and portages. Stopping places are rare!

SECTION B

4 km of Class IV-V   Kayaking ★ ★   Scenery ★ ★

Put In
Put in at the take as above.

Take Out
This is either at the confluence with the Salat or continue down the Salat (see above).

Description
Watch out for fallen trees in this narrow river.

L'Arac

12 km of Class II-III D   Kayaking ★★   Scenery ★★

The River
The Arac is a right bank tributary of the Salat entering near **Kercabanac**. Principally fed by rainwater but aided by the late April early May thaw.

Put In - at the village of Biert on the D 618.

Take Out
Use the confluence with the Salat at Kercabanac.

Description
A pleasant paddle, hindered by trees here and there. The only dam can be shot on the right.

Le Garbet

The River
The Garbet offers water at a similar time to those already described above. The single minor water abstraction hardly affects the water level. The outlet for the above can be seen from the road.

SECTION A (from Aulus-les-Bains to Erce)
8 km of Class III-IV (5) E D   Kayaking ★★   Scenery ★★

Put In
At **Aulus-Les-Bains** on the D 32 from Oust.

Take Out - At the village of Erce again on the D 32.

Description
The gorges around halfway present the most difficulties in an otherwise wide valley. This difficult stretch can be examined on foot from the right above the hamlet of **Les Escales**. A second rapid after the gorges can spring as a surprise on the unwary particularly if exhausted by the earlier effort.

SECTION B (from Erce to Oust)
7 km of Class III (4)   Kayaking ★★   Scenery ★★

Put In - At Les Escales just above Erce.

Take Out
This is at the approach to **Oust** but an easier option is to proceed into the Salat but you should note that two dams in Oust will then need to be negotiated.

Description
This is a run which twists around a lot and requires lots of manoeuvring.

L'Alet

The River

This river begins at the confluence of the Cors and the Ossesse and like others has a season mid May to mid June. The Alet joins the Salat at **Pont-de-la-Taule**. A minor water abstraction between St.-Lizie-d'Ustou and Serac-d'Oustou has little effect on water level.

SECTION A   (from Stillom to St. Lizier d'Ustou)

2.5 km of Class III (5)   Kayaking ★★   Scenery ★★

Put In

Stillom (Estillon) lies 2 km up the valley from Ustou on the D38. Put in just below the confluence of the Cors and Ossesse slightly downstream of the village.

Take Out

At the barrage 200m upstream of St.-Lizier-d'Oustou.

Description

This is mainly a pleasant but technical descent, however the Class 5 stretch should be scouted on the way up the valley. This is downstream from the village of Portet and consists of a rock sill which bars exit from a pretty gorge. The portage on the right bank is 'delicat'!

(We haven't managed to get around to running the stretch below the barrage at the take out. This looks an interesting gorge (perhaps Class IV?) which can be viewed from the right bank).

SECTION B   (from Serac-d'Ustou to Pont de la Taule)

8 km of Class II-III-IV   Kayaking ★★★   Scenery ★★

Put In

From Pont de la Taule keep on the D 8 towards Guzet to put in at the bridge just below **Serac d'Oustou.**

Take Out

On the left bank at **Pont de la Taule** just before the confluence with the Salat. It is quite possible to continue the descent down the Salat - see above.

Description

The first few kilometres give a quiet start amid lovely scenery, the more serious rapids begin near the hamlet of la Pomarede and continue on down requiring some enjoyable paddling at good water levels.

Note that near the take out there is a cable used formerly to pull wood across the river. This should be noted but is easy to avoid.

Le Cors (or Upper Alet)

4 km of Class IV-V (6)   Kayaking ★★   Scenery ★★

The River
The Cors joins the Ossesse at **Stillom** (Estillon) to form the Alet which is itself an important tributary of the Salat. The valley itself is unspoilt by tourism and has a certain charm.

Rain and thaw from about mid may to early June give the best period for paddling. There are no hydroelectric installations.

Put In
From Pont-de-la-Taule take the D 8 towards the Col de Latrape. After the village of Le Trein d'Ustou take the D 38 to the right towards St. Lizier d'Ustou to the village of Stillom (Estillon). From there take the left fork towards the **Cirque de Cagateille.** Access is at the end of this stretch of road.

Take Out
At the road bridge at Stillom (Estillon).

Description
This run is similar in style to the Riberot - the descent is technical and continuous between granite blocks. The first part is canyon-like and 'tres virulent' at high water and the first 100 m should be scouted before setting off. The rest of the run is less of a problem in high water but all the same beware of some of the drops.

Le Cors ou Haut Alet.

Clément sur le parcours supérieur de la Cinqueta.

Río Baliera, "parcours B".

"Partie classique" du rio Cinqueta.

Barranco de Viu, magnifique lorsqu'on retrouve l'eau.

La vallée du río Baliera, étroite et profonde...

Bassin de l'Ariège

Tourist Offices

www.ariegepyrenees.com

AUZAT-VICDESSOS (09220)
OFFICE DE TOURISME
Rue des Pyrénées
09220 AUZAT
Tél : 05.61.64.87.53, Fax : 05.61.03.82.05

AX-LES-THERMES (09250)
OFFICE DE TOURISME
6, rue de la Mairie
09250 LUZENAC
Tél : 05.61.64.60.60, Fax : 05.61.64.41.08,

FOIX (09000)
OFFICE DE TOURISME
45, cours Gabriel Fauré - BP 20
Tél : 05.61.65.12.12, Fax : 05.61.65.64.63

LAVELANET (09300)
OFFICE DE TOURISME
Maison de Lavelanet - BP 89
Tél : 05.61.01.22.20, Fax : 05.61.03.06.39

TARASCON-SUR-ARIEGE (09400)
OFFICE DE TOURISME
Avenue des Pyrénées - BP 33
Tél :05.61.05.94.94, Fax : 05.61.05.57.79

Rafting & Kayak Companies

Passeur de Vagues
09140 Seix
Tel : 05 61 66 84 88

Riverside
Mondin Thierry
09400 Saurat, Foix
Tel : 05 61 05 14 06

BASSIN DE L'ARIÈGE

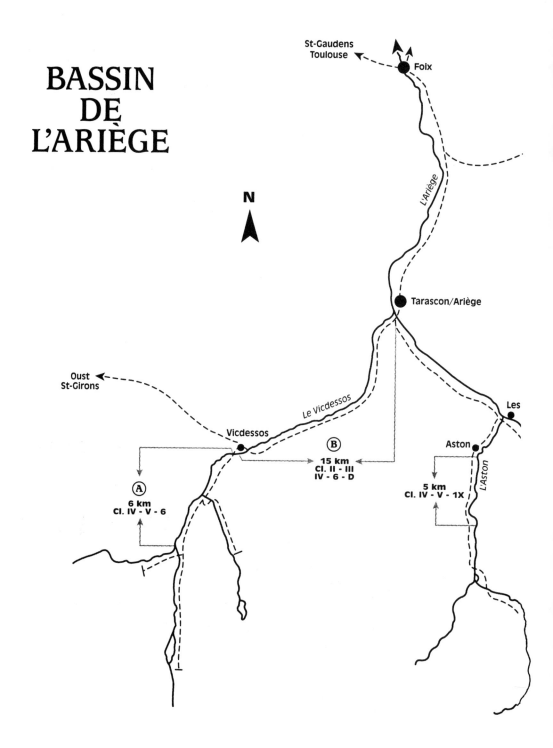

N

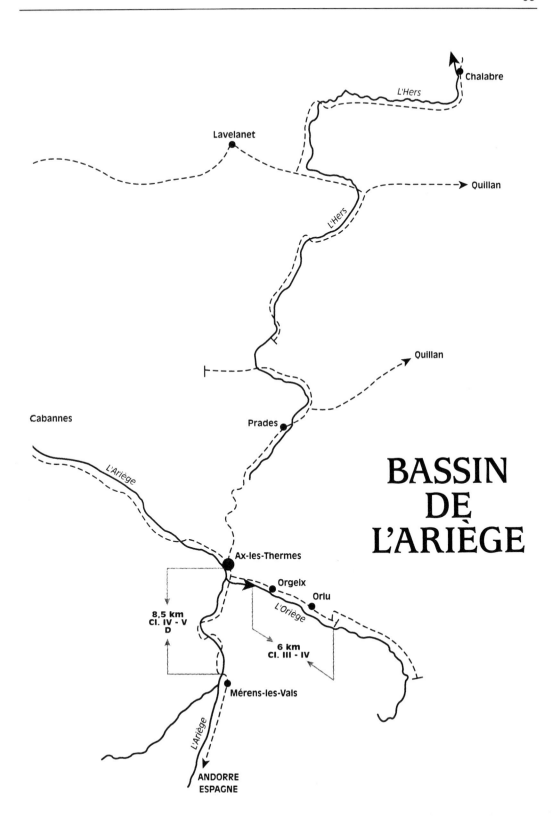

L'Hers

Chalabre

Lavelanet

L'Hers

Quillan

Quillan

Cabannes

Prades

L'Ariège

BASSIN DE L'ARIÈGE

Ax-les-Thermes

Orgeix

Orlu

L'Oriège

**8,5 km
Cl. IV - V
D**

**6 km
Cl. III - IV**

Mérens-les-Vals

L'Ariège

**ANDORRE
ESPAGNE**

L'Ariège

8.5 km of class IV-V D   Kayaking ★★   Scenery ★★

The River
The Ariège is fed by rain and melt water but unfortunately its course is interrupted by large hydro-electric installations. The section described can be paddled during the thaw period thanks to influx of water from tributaries joining the Ariège near the village of Mérens-les-Vals.

Put In
At the first road bridge about 800 m downstream of **Mérens-les-Vals.**

Take Out
This is in the village of **Ax-les-Thermes**. Take the direction towards the ski centre of Ax-Bonascre, cross the Ariège and leave the vehicles in the car park on the left bank.

Description
Soon after putting in you come across a lovely fall of about 3 m that can be shot or portaged on the left bank. After a further drop the river steadies down before the first road bridge. The drops can normally be shot after inspection and the road runs along the right bank. We are now in the thick of a succession of continuous large rapids.

At the start of the last third of the section a dam can be inspected and if necessary portaged by the left bank. Beware of fallen trees which might require portage.

L'Oriège

6 km of class III-IV   Kayaking ★★   Scenery ★★

The River
The Oriège depends upon rain and melt water. It is best paddled during the thaw from mid-May to mid-June or in periods of heavy rain.

Put in
On the southern edge of **Ax-les-Thermes** take the D 22 on the left towards **Orlu**. Go through the village and carry on through to the large car park at the next village of Forges d'Orlu, some 3 km further on and put in here.

Take out - at the dam visible from the road, just downstream from the village of **Orgeix**.

Description
The greatest difficulties are concentrated in the half of the section before you reach Orlu when the river is both big and technical. From here until the dam the river becomes much easier, class II+ (3).

Beware of trees on all of this run.

For the record
We also tried a higher section when we had a good water level. To access this take the road on the left just before Forges d'Orlu and drive to the car park. This section gives you 3 good km of class IV to V, very continuous but with some trees. Watch out as you arrive at Forges d'Orlu, the river falls drastically.

Le Vicdessos

The River

The Vicdessos is a left bank tributary of the of the Ariège, flowing into it at the village of **Tarascon**, 16 km upstream of Foix. It is mainly fed by snows from the valley slopes of the mountain peak of Montcalm (3078 m). Unfortunately, paddling is only possible during the thaw and when water is released from the dam at Pla de Soulcem.

SECTION A   (from Montcalm to Auzat)

6 km of class IV-V (6)   Kayaking ★★   Scenery ★★

Put In

The put in is under the little road bridge leading to the hamlet of **Montcalm** just before where the D 108 crosses the D 66.

Take Out

It is better to take out a few hundred metres upstream from the road bridge at the exit from the village of **Auzat**.

Description

In the first half of the river, the Vicdessos has some straightforward drops which give way gradually to steep, technical rapids typical of the Pyrenees.

We didn't shoot the last fall under the road bridge (about 4 m) because of the difficulty of having bank safety support even though the drop seemed feasible.

SECTION B   (from Auzat to Tarascon)

15 km of class II-III-IV (6) D   Kayaking ★   Scenery ★

Put In

In the village of Auzat take the road towards the camp site on the left going back along the valley. The put in is below the road bridge just before the camp site.

Take Out

The take out is at the confluence of the Vicdessos and the Ariège at **Tarascon** or below the road bridge on the N 20.

Description

Most of the descent is class II-III. The river is fairly wide and rapids with small waves are interspersed with more rock strewn passages. Just upstream from Laramade a pressure pipeline crosses the river, signalling the first class 6 rapid which can be carried on the left bank. The following 200 m are class 4 and lead directly to the second grade 6 which is best portaged right. The river then remains class IV for a few hundred metres before calming down to class II–III. For the last kilometre beware of currents carrying you into the undercut limestone rock faces.

A dam in the village of **Vicdessos** can be carried on the left bank and another, downstream from the village of **Niaux** and visible from the road can be shot or carried on the left bank.

L'Aston

5 km of class IV-V (x)   Kayaking ★★   Scenery ★★

The River

The Aston is a tributary of the left bank of the Ariège, flowing into it at the village of **Cabannes**. The best time for paddling is during the thaw period, in May and June. Even then it is very uncertain, being dependent on water releases from the dam at Riete.

To get a good idea of the water level you need to look at the river upstream from the village of **Aston** because water is put back into the river just below this village.

Put In

From **Aston** drive up the valley for about 6 km to where the river appears from a gorge. Put in here.

Take Out -

The take out is 200 m upstream from **Aston** village where the road is closest to the river.

Description

This gorge starts with a big rapid that we have rated as un-runnable for some 12 years. There is a series of drops needing bank support in place. The first part of this section is canyon-like and not visible from the road but it is possible to scout it on foot on the left bank. The rapid we rate as impossible comes after the canyon just upstream from a footpath at the side of the road.

A little further on make sure you scout a large drop sometimes visible from the road depending on how thick the vegetation is. Following this is a group of rapids which are problem-free and linger fondly in the memory. The road follows the river along its length and access is easy if there are problems.

For the record

We think it is probably possible paddle the river upstream of this section - it appears to have a similar technical character.

Bassin Mediterranean

Tourist Offices

AMELIE-LES-BAINS-PALALDA (66110)
OFFICE DE TOURISME
Quai du 8 mai 1945 -
Tél : 04.68.39.01.98, Fax : 04.68.39.20.20,

PRATS-DE-MOLLO-LA-PRESTE
OFFICE DE TOURISME
EL FIRAL
Tél : 04.68.39.70.83, Fax : 04.68.39.74.51

ILLE-SUR-TET (66130)
OFFICE DE TOURISME
Square de la Poste - BP 14
Tél : 0468.84.02.62, Fax : 04.68.84.16.10

PRADES (66500)
OFFICE DE TOURISME
4, rue Victor Hugo
Tél :04.68.05.41.02, Fax : 04.68.05.21.79,

QUILLAN (11500)
OFFICE DE TOURISME
Place de la Gare
Tél : 04.68.20.07.78, Fax : 04.68.20.04.91

LIMOUX (11300)
OFFICE DE TOURISME
Promenade du Tivoli
Tél : 04.68.31.11.82, Fax : 04.68.31.87.14

PERPIGNAN (66002)
OFFICE DE TOURISME
Palais des Congrès
Plac Armand Lanoux - BP 215
Tél : 04.68.66.30.30, Fax : 04.68.66.30.26

Rafting & Kayak Companies

La Forge Sports Centre International
Route Perpignan (Camping la Forge)
11500 **Quillan**
Tel : 04 68 20 23 79, Fax : 04 68 20 13 64

Sud Rafting
Base de Loisirs
Pont d'Alies a **Axat**
Tel : 04 68 20 53 73, Fax : 04 68 20 62 38

Association Pyrene
Camping du Pont d'Alies
11140 **Axat**
Tel : 04 68 20 52 76

Alet Eaux Vives
11580 **Alet les Bains**
Tel : 04 68 69 92 67

Embarquement Immediat
Hameau des Sauzils
11260 **Fa.**
Tel : 04 68 20 18 45

Alies Aventure
Place de l'Eglise
11500 **St. Martin Lys**
Tel : 04 68 20 96 59

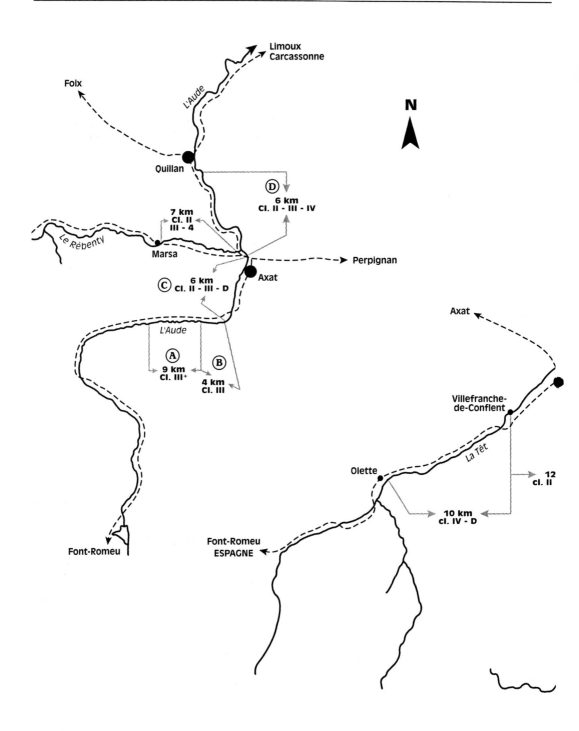

BASSIN MÉDITERRANÉEN

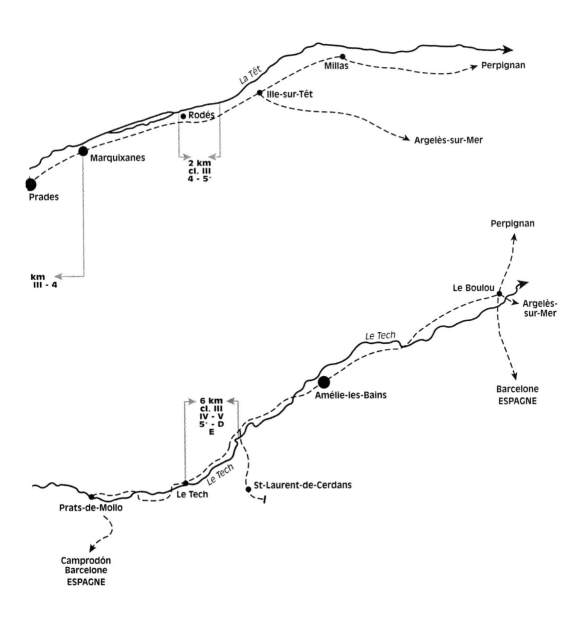

L'Aude

The River

The Aude has fairly extensive valley slopes with summits reaching 2700 m. Two large dams limit the effects of the thaw however they do mean that there are water releases which normally allow **paddling throughout the summer.**

Sections A and B rarely have enough water and to paddle them you need to make use of the releases from the hydro-electric stations or be there when its raining heavily.

It's easier to find good water levels on sections C and D thanks to the presence of numerous power stations. The 'Defile de Pierre-Lys' can be run during most of the Summer season.

SECTION A

9 km of class III+   Kayaking ★★   Scenery ★

Put In

The put in is at the hydro-electric station on the D 118 at the junction of the crossing towards the village of **Campagna de Sault**.

Take out

This is at the next hydro-electric station (Centrale de **Gesse**) 9 km downstream.

Description

This is a pleasant section to paddle and the steady gradient doesn't allow you to get bored. Always be wary of trees and, at high water levels, it might be better to scout for their possible presence from the road which runs along the river all the way.

SECTION B (from Gesse to Nantilla)

4 km of class III   Kayaking ★★   Scenery ★

Put In

The put in is at the hydro-electric station at **Gesse** 1 km downstream from the village.

Take Out

This is at the hydro-electric station at Nantilla.

Description

This section is very similar to the previous one involving a technical descent. The road is always close and you must watch out for trees.

SECTION C (from Nantilla to Axat)

6 km of class III-III D   Kayaking ★★   Scenery ★

Put In

At the hydro-electric station at **Nantilla**

Take Out

The take out is at the edge of the village of **Axat** at the road bridge of Alies.

Description

This is a narrow, technical run with no particular hazards apart from a small **weir** just upstream from the village of Axat that can form a real stopper at high water.

SECTION D   (Defile de Pierre-Lys)

6 km of class II-III-IV   Kayaking ★ ★   Scenery ★ ★

Put In

A the end of the village of Axat at the road bridge of Alies.

Take Out

At the end of the Pierre-Lys Gorge.

Description

This popular run has no particular difficulties and the road follows it all the way. The class IV rapids are clustered in the narrow gorge of Pierre-Lys and so are visible from the road.

For your information there is a gauge on the road bridge that leads to St Martin-Lys. 70 cm indicates a medium water level.

Le Rébenty

7 km of class II-III (4)   Kayaking ★   Scenery ★

The River

Paddling on the Rébenty is mostly done after heavy rainfall.

Put In

The put in is 500 m downstream from the village of **Marsa** below the water outflow.

Take Out

The take out is just before the confluence of the Rébenty and the Aude.

Description

The Rébenty is a narrow river with only slight gradient, flowing quietly between wooded banks. The road follows the river along its length and gives you the chance of scouting the class 4 rapid before attempting it. This rapid is about two-thirds of the way down the run and can be easily portaged.

La Têt

2 km of class III (4) (5+)   Kayaking ★★   Scenery ★★

The River

The Têt is fed from rain and melt water but the whole course of the river is affected by a large number of barrages all the way up to the highest reaches. We have deliberately not described the old 'classic' sections where the paddling is now very uncertain because of these dams. For your information these run from Olette to Villefranche de Conflent (10 km class IV D) and from Villefranche de Conflent to Marquixans (12 km class II-III (4)). For any chance of paddling these sections choose periods when it is raining on the snow or during the height of the thaw around the end of May.

The section described below can be paddled for most of the year thanks to water releases from the large dam at Vinca.

Put In

Driving on the N 116 a little way downstream from the village of Vinca take the road to the village of **Rodes**. On entering the village take a narrow road on the left that leads to the foot of the dam where you can put in.

Take Out

Take out from the river by carrying your kayak about 50 m when you reach the dam (at the end of the difficult stretch) and then put in again and paddle along an irrigation canal that takes you directly to the side of the main road.

By car, take the main road from Rodes in the direction of Perpignan and 2 km further just after the railways take a road to the left through orchards. You will pass over an irrigation canal where the take out is made.

Description

This run cuts through a **magnificent gorge of white granite** and the river is fairly narrow. The first 500 m up to the road bridge at Rodes is class II. After that there are pronounced rapids, especially a double drop that you shoot on the left with a **siphon** at the exit, particularly dangerous if you swim.

The gorge has a foot path along it, running high up along the right bank and this is useful for scouting and portaging.

Le Tech

6 km of class III-IV-V (5+) E   Kayaking ★★   Scenery ★★

The River

The best time to paddle this river is after the heavy rainfalls of Autumn or in the thaw during Spring (However when there is snow, there is not usually much, so the thaw rarely gives adequate water levels). This lack of reliable water, and its geographical isolation means that this river is not paddled very often. This is a pity because the 'Grande Gorge du Tech' would otherwise be of great interest to kayakers.

Put In

This is in the village of **le Tech.**

Take Out

Abut 1 km upstream from **Can Parterre** (which is 5 km upstream from d'Arles sur Tech) leave the D 115 and turn to the right along the D 3 which leads to St Laurent de Cerdans. A small steep climb leads out of the gorge at the road bridge.

Description

Up to the water extraction point in the middle of the run the rapids are class III followed by class IV. After that the river becomes canyon-like again and the descent becomes class V. Where the river narrows is a class 5+ rapid which requires a stop for reflection!

The gorge is extremely beautiful with pronounced rapids in a wonderful setting.

Nigel suddenly spots his excuse ....

Bassin du Río Aragon

Tourist Offices

www.cfnavarra.es

Pamplona
Servicio de Turismo
31005 Pamplona
Tel : 948 42 77 53
Fax : 948 42 35 97

OCHAGAVIA
TORISMO
31680 Ochagavia
Tel : 948 89 06 41
Fax : 948 89 06 79

RONCAL
TORISMO
31415 Roncal
Tel/Fax : 948 47 52 56

AYERBE
TORISMO
Plaza de Aragón, 40
Tel : 974 38 00 25

PUENTE LA REINA
TORISMO
Cruce Ctra. Jaca-Pamplona
Tel : 974 37 72 01

JACA
TORISMO
Regimiento de Galicia, 2
Tél : 974 36 00 89

Rafting & Kayak Companies

Nattura
Pamplona, Tel : 948 13 10 44
Murillo de Gallego, Tel : 974 38 30 91
email : nattura@masbytes.es

EKiA
Camping Osate
31680 Otsagabia
Tel : 948 89 01 84

Alcorce Pirineos Aventura
Regimiento Galicia 1
22700 Jaca
Tel : 34 974 356 437
Fax : 974 363 972
www.alcorceaventura.com

1. BASSIN DU RÍO ARAGON

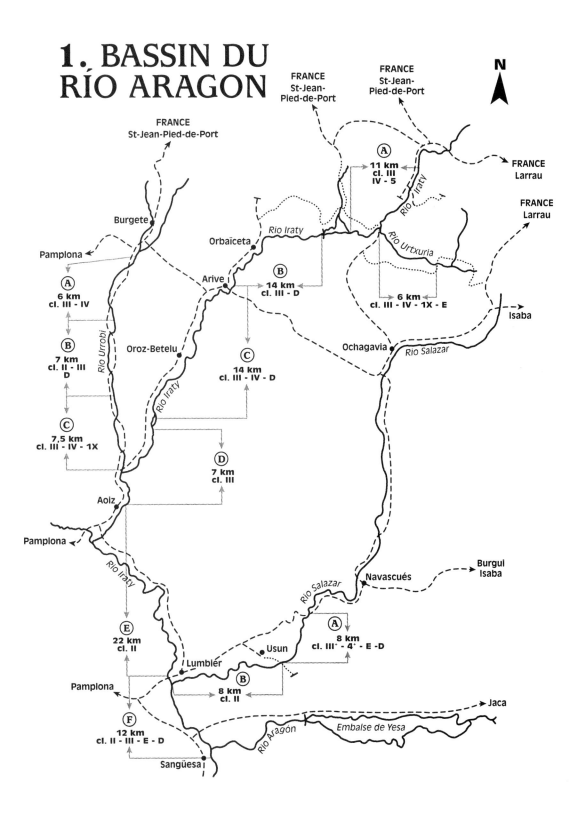

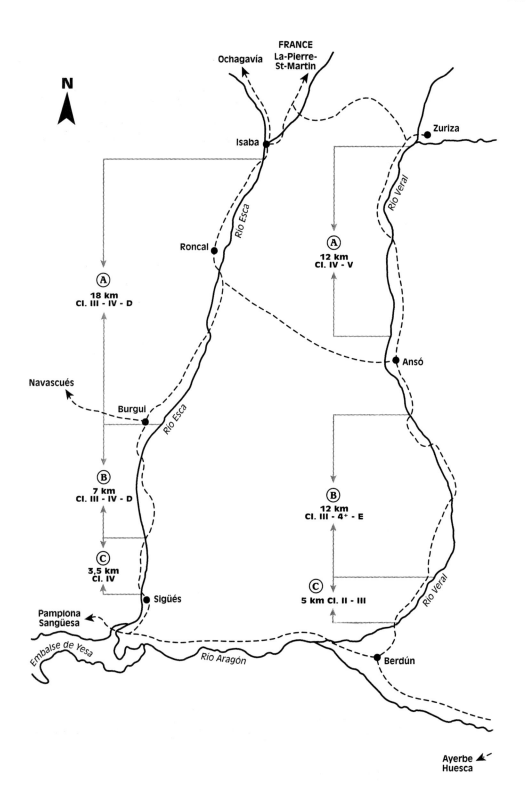

FRANCE
La-Pierre-
St-Martin

Ochagavía

Zuriza

N

Isaba

Río Veral

Río Esca

Roncal

(A)
12 km
Cl. IV - V

(A)
18 km
Cl. III - IV - D

Ansó

Navascués

Burgui

Río Esca

(B)
7 km
Cl. III - IV - D

(B)
12 km
Cl. III - 4⁺ - E

(C)
3,5 km
Cl. IV

(C)
5 km Cl. II - III

Río Veral

Sigüés

Pamplona
Sangüesa

Embalse de Yesa

Río Aragón

Berdún

Ayerbe
Huesca

2. BASSIN DU RÍO ARAGON

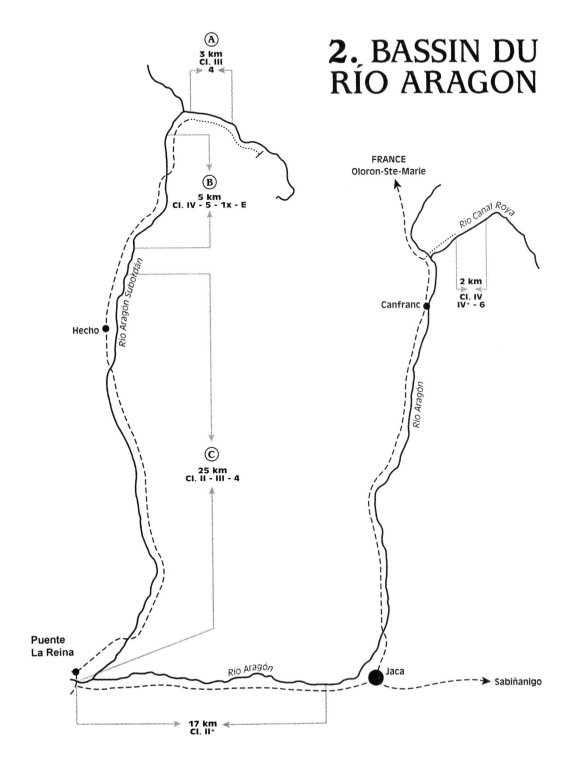

Ⓐ
3 km
Cl. III
4

Ⓑ
5 km
Cl. IV - 5 - 1x - E

Ⓒ
25 km
Cl. II - III - 4

Hecho

Río Aragón Subordán

Puente
La Reina

Río Aragón

17 km
Cl. II⁺

FRANCE
Oloron-Ste-Marie

Río Canal Roya

2 km
Cl. IV
IV⁺ - 6

Canfranc

Río Aragón

Jaca

Sabiñanigo

Río Urrobi

The River

The Urrobi is the principal tributary of the Rio Iraty. It relies mainly on a rainwater catchment and is viable for paddling during autumn and winter.

The level can be judged from the water gauge above the village of Burgete (see location below) :

40 cm - the minimum to attempt Section A. 60 cm - the rapids need some scouting prior to descent.

80 cm - the descent is unforgiving and Section A will be Class V+ at this level.

SECTION A

6 km of Class III-IV (see above)   Kayaking ★★   Scenery ★★

Put In

From the N 135 turn off 2.5 km below **Auritz-Burguete** and take the NA 172 which then starts to follow the river along this section. The little house alongside the river has the scale referred to above and the put in is made nearby.

Take Out - at the bridge on the side road left off the NA 172 leading to the village of **Arrieta**.

Description

There are no major difficulties but note that the flow is more sustained during the second part of the run.

SECTION B (from Arrieta to Arce)

7 km of Class II-III D   Kayaking ★   Scenery ★

Put In - at **Arrietta** - see above.

Take Out

At the road bridge over the river on the side road left off the NA 172/C 127 leading to the village of **Arce**.

Description

There is a fish farm below the bridge at Arrieta with a dam which is not shootable. There is then a difficult stretch down to the above take out where the vegetation makes paddling problematical. This section is thus not particularly useful and may even pose dangers.

SECTION C (from Arce to the Rio Iraty)

7.5 km of Class III-IV (x)   Kayaking ★   Scenery ★

Put In - at the road bridge at **Arce** (see above).

Take Out

7 km below Arce take the NA 204 to the left towards **Aribe**. The take out is at the road bridge soon after turning off the C 127.

Description

There is fast flow and the paddling is continuous. The impassable bit is between the two road bridges on the C 127. This is followed by an attractive gorge of Class IV which becomes much more difficult in high water. The river is then Class II to the take out.

N.B. A barrage is planned near Itoiz which would wipe out this section.

Río Iraty

The River
Starting in France within the forest of the same name, the Iraty can be paddled during the mid April thaw but even then is best supported by heavy rain.

SECTION A (high)
11 km of Class III-IV (5)   Kayaking ★★   Scenery ★★★

Put In
In France, from Larrau on the D 26 take the D 19 over the Col de Bagargui and continue the descent towards St Jean Pied de Port for some 6 km. Then take the left turn onto the D 18 to access the river at **Chalet Pedro**.

Take Out
Take the left turn onto the D 301 about 600 m upstream of Pedro Chalet. 5.5 km along this road towards St. Jean Pied de Port turn off left and due South into the valley of the Rio Urrio. Keep to this road until it peters out into a track and after 1 km cross a ford to arrive at a junction. Turn left here and leave the vehicles when above the lake, or if desired leave a vehicle 6 km upstream at the confluence of the Rio Iraty and Rio Urtxuria to take out there.

Description
The gorge bit is 'tres sympathique' with lots of technical bits but only one drop to cause problems in high water., the drops in the gorges only normally cause problems in high water. The 11 km run has pleasant scenery with a 4 km Class II-III stretch between the confluence with the Urtxuria and the lake.

The river above the confluence is sometimes called the Rio Urbeltza. Allow 40 minutes to take the vehicles from the Put In to the lake if the whole section is to be attempted - the shuttle to the confluence is about half of this.

SECTION B (from Irabia Barrage to Arive)
14 km of Class III D   Kayaking ★★   Scenery ★★

Put in
Below the barrage at the western end of the lake - this is called the Embalse de Irabiako.

Take Out
At the village of **Arive** on the NA 203.

Description
Spanish kayakers tell us that one barrage may cause problems in high water.

SECTION C (from Arive to Artozqui)
14 km of Class III-IV D   Kayaking ★★   Scenery ★

Put In
At Arive.

Take Out
At the lake before the dam at **Artozqui**.

Description

On leaving Arive the river picks up momentum to give Class III rapids between flat stretches. The first barrage has a slide at the centre which is best examined before attempting to shoot.

Level with the village of **Oladea** another dam can be shot but only via the slide at the left. From here there is the **great classic run** of the Iraty with Class IV rapids and only rarely more gentle stretches.

Following this there are two other barrages and a pretty section adjacent to the road. After **Oroz Betelu** there are two more barrages which can be negotiated in moderate water, and then the remainder of the run is pleasant with some Class III rapids.

SECTION D (from the barrage at Usoz to Aoiz)

7 km of Class III   Kayaking ★★   Scenery ★

Put In

On the left bank at the base of the barrage at Usoz. Cross by the suspension bridge.

Take Out

Level with the village of Aoiz.

Description

The biggest rapid is encountered just after the Put In and then the rest of the runs is Class II-III.

*N.B. A **projected barrage at Itoiz** will wipe out the lower part of this run near the confluence with the Urrobi which itself will be affected.*

SECTION E (from Aoiz to Lumbier)

22 km of Class II   Kayaking ★★   Scenery ★

Put In - At Aoiz

Take Out

At the road bridge at the edge of the village of **Lumbier**.

Description

After the confluence with the Urrobi there is much more water but the rapids do not exceed Class II and are spaced out by flat stretches.

SECTION F (from Lumbier to Sanguesa)

12 km of Class II-III E D   Kayaking ★★   Scenery ★★

Put In

At the previous take out.

Take Out

Level with the village of Sanguesa.

Description

There are mostly no difficulties in paddling this beautiful deep gorge. A barrage about half way through the gorge is normally negotiated on the right and this is followed by a pretty Class III rapid which leads to the exit of the gorge.

A little above Sanguesa the Iraty joins the Aragon, the river loses her name, her power, and character.

Río Urtxuria

6 km of Class III-IV (x) E　　　　　　　　　Kayaking ★★★　　Scenery ★★★

The River
This Basque river is only viable after periods of rain.

Put In
In France take the D 26 from Larrau to Port Larrau and after the minor tunnel descend another 3 km to a bar at **Abodi** which doubles as a Cross Country Ski Centre. Take the track to the right here which leads to the river after some 8.5 km. Put on below the bridge.

Take Out
Carry on along the track which follows the river down from the Put In to join a tarmac road after some 7 km. Turn right along the latter to get to the confluence with the Rio Iraty. You can taket out here or continue down the Iraty for a further 4 km of Class II-III to the lake. The track is found again well along the lake on the right.

Description
This is a magnificent run through little gorges and with well-defined Class IV rapids. The river flows through some dense forest and trees will present a hazard. The road is some distance away from the river.
The time needed for shuttle from the road bridge to the confluence is about 20 minutes.

Río Urrobi.

Río Salazar

The River

The Rio Salazar has a large catchment containing peaks up to 1500 m and can be kayaked in rainy periods. There are no hydro-electric plants on the sections described.

SECTION A (from Pont de Biguesa to Usun)

8 km of Class III+ (4+) E D   Kayaking ★★   Scenery ★★★

Put In

The put in is 8 km down the Salazar valley from the village of **Navasques** at the road bridge (there is a left turn towards Biguezal at this point).

Take Out

Carry on from the Put In towards Lumbier and at Domeno take a right turn to Usun. Here take the track to a submerged bridge which is the put in point.

Description

This is a beautiful section with vultures, cliffs and a wild river. The Class 4+ rapid has a dangerous stopper at the exit of the gorge. After a further 50 m and about 500 m above the Take Out at Usun you must portage on the left to avoid an artificial construction - this is not easy and may require using ropes. The remainder of the run is without difficulty.

SECTION B (from the bridge at Usun to Lumbier)

8 km of Class II   Kayaking ★   Scenery ★

Put In

At the previous take out.

Take Out

At the confluence with the Rio Iraty at Lumbier.

Description

The river has become larger, slower and is less enclosed so it is not therefore as attractive as higher up.

If wanted you can continue the run down into the Iraty - with water not exceeding Class III - see Section F of that river.

Río Esca

The River

The Rio Esca is one the main western flowing rivers where thaw affects whether you can paddle or not. Nevertheless the medium altitude catchment normally gives sufficient water during later April and during periods of heavy rain.

SECTION A   (from Isaba to Burgui)

18 km of Class III-IV D   Kayaking ★ ★   Scenery ★ ★

Put In

At the road bridge downstream of the village of **Isaba**.

Take Out

Level with the village of **Burgui**.

Description

The flow is more sustained above **Roncal**. The dams which abstract water and hinder descent can be seen from the road which hugs the river. The first two can be shot via a slide but the barrage at Roncal must be portaged on the left.

SECTION B   (from Burgui to Salvatierra)

7 km of Class III-IV D   Kayaking ★ ★   Scenery ★ ★

Put In

At the take out above.

Take Out

At the road bridge downstream of **Salvatierra**.

Description

The road follows the river for two thirds of the run. The one small water intake dam can usually be shot.

SECTION C   (from Salvatierra to Sigues)

3.5 km of Class IV   Kayaking ★ ★   Scenery ★ ★

Put In

At the take out above.

Take Out

At the road bridge at **Sigues**.

Description

This is undoubtedly the **best run** on the river with good rapids and strong eddies. (From Sigues to the barrage of Yesa is about 2-3 km - the river mellows out and the going is easy).

There is a water gauge at Sigues - 0.4 seems the minimum and 1.65 the maximum levels for paddling.

Río Veral

The River

Arising near the peak of Ansabere (2400 m) the Rio Veral is fed by contributions from early April thaw and rainfall. There are no hydro-electric stations throughout the 50 km journey to the Aragon.

SECTION A (upper)

12 km of Class IV-V   Kayaking ★★★   Scenery ★★★

Put In

One road alone (HU 2024) goes up the valley of the Veral. The put in is near **Zuriza** where the more major NA 200 enters the valley.

Take Out

This is 1.5 km above the village of **Anso** near the road bridge leading to a farm.

Description

This run is in a beautiful valley with limestone cliffs. The first 5 km is very technical and continuous, with the uncertainty of the unknown around every bend. After the only road bridge between Anso and Zuriza the river becomes somewhat easier but still keeps you on your toes.

SECTION B (middle)

12 km of Class III (4+) E   Kayaking ★★   Scenery ★★

Put In

At the first road bridge 3 km downstream of **Anso**.

Take Out

17 km down from Anso and before the road gets narrower.

Description

From the first to the second road bridge there is a 1 km stretch of Class II with a Class 4 rapid. The river here is gorge like but the road is nearby. Then after the second road bridge and down to the third bridge is a 5 km section of Class II.

   After the third bridge there is an excellent 6 km of Class III (4) in a magnificent locked-in canyon. The Class 4 rapid passage is at the start of this stretch.

SECTION C (lower)

5 km of Class II-III   Kayaking ★★   Scenery ★★★

Put In

50m downstream of the take out above. Portage the new dam on the right to put in below.

Take Out

5 km further downstream at the road bridge.

Description

For the first 2 km the river runs busily through a pretty gorge from which it then it abruptly emerges to flow tranquilly across a flat plain.

Río Aragón Subordán

The River

This river flows in a valley which is similar and parallel to the Rio Veral - again with no hydro-electric barrages to hinder passage.

SECTION A (upper)

3 km of Class III (4)   Kayaking ★ ★   Scenery ★ ★ ★

Put In

Only one road follows the valley to become a track with the access point some 3 km further on along the latter.

Take Out

Level with the large parking area at the start of the above track.

Description

This is a magnificent run with a backdrop of mountains and rolling countryside. The river is narrow and gorge-like in places with a mix of easy and more difficult rapids. It has some tricky stretches but stops are possible in between.

SECTION B (The Red Gorge)

5 km of Class IV (5) (x) E   Kayaking ★ ★   Scenery ★ ★

Put In

This is where the road joins the river about 15 km above the village of **Hecho** or if desired somewhat higher at the previous take out.

Take Out

Before the ravine visible from the road about 10 km above Hecho, a little above the 'Boca del Infierno'.

Description

After the first rapid there is a dangerous drop at the entrance to the gorge formed by an un-runnable ledge - a portage is best made via the road to put in again below as soon as practicable.

(At low water the 'Boca del Infierno' has been been run but the drops are undercut and kayaks and paddlers can end up trapped behind the waterfall.)

SECTION C (from La Boca to the Rio Aragon)

25 km of Class II-III (4)   Kayaking ★ ★   Scenery ★ ★

Put In

Driving up the valley on the H 2131 there is a small road to the right about 1 km below the 'Boca del Infierno' which leads to a bridge. The rapid at the bridge has been paddled but it is easier to put in below.

Take Out

At the road bridge at Puente la Reina

Description

This section is interesting in good water with excellent waves and a good current. The Class 4 rapid is a 2 m drop about 2.5 km above Embun. After Embun the gradient moderates to give only Class II rapids.

Río Aragón Subordán.

Río Aragón

17 km of Class II+   Kayaking ★   Scenery ★★

The River

The Rio Aragon is fed by thaws in late April to early May. The upper section between Canfranc and Jaca is spoilt by numerous barrages so we have been discouraged from investigating this section.

Below Jaca the river is free flowing.

Put In

This is 3 km downstream of Jaca where the road to Pamplona meets the river.

Take Out

Following the road to Pamplona you can take out 20 km below Jaca at the road bridge of Puente-la-Reina .

Description

This is a pleasant paddle in the Spanish sunshine with a few Class II rapids to entertain and distract you from enjoying the beautiful countryside.

Río Canal Roya

2 km of Class IV-IV+ (6)   Kayaking ★   Scenery ★

The River

This small tributary enters the left bank of the Aragon downstream of **Candanchu**. The catchment thaws around the end of April to mid May and descent during rainy periods may also be well possible.

Put In

From France via the Col du Somport on the N 134 descend the now E 7/ N 330 to soon pass a military barracks at a bend to the right. Take the dirt road to the left to go up the valley of the Canal Roya and at the end of this one has to carry on by foot down a path for some 20 minutes to reach the put in point at a bridge.

Take Out

2 km downstream above a rough rocky stretch.

Description

This run is set in the midst of magnificent mountain scenery and at the heart of an open valley. At the two thirds stage it is judicious to get out at the bridge to closely inspect the next 50 m which contain a Class 6 rapid - best portaged on the left.

The remaining stretch is Class IV+ to the take out.

Bassin Río Gállego

Tourist Offices

www.cfnavarra.es

JACA
TORISMO
Regimiento de Galicia, 2
Tél : 974 36 00 89

SABIÑANIGO
TORISMO
Plaza de España 2
Tél : 974 48 00 05

HUESCA
TORISMO
Coso Alto 23
Tel : 974 23 22 57 78

Rafting & Kayak Companies

Nattura
Pamplona, Tel : 948 13 10 44
Murillo de Gállego, Tel : 974 38 30 91
email : nattura@masbytes.es

Alcorce Pirineos Aventura
Regimiento Galicia 1
22700 Jaca
Tel : 34 974 356 437
Fax : 974 363 972
www.alcorceaventura.com

Río Gállego.

BASSIN
RÍO GÁLLEGO

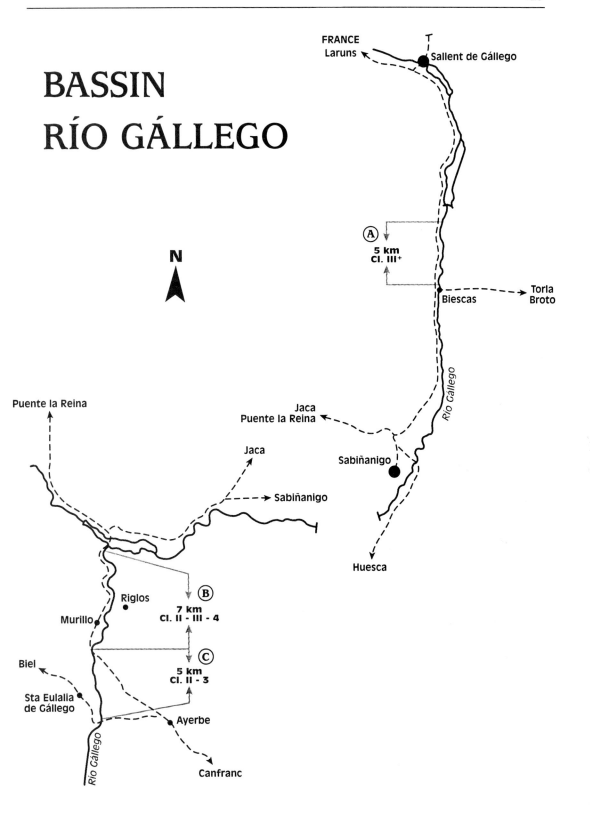

Rio Gállego

The River

This left bank tributary of the Rio Ebro joins the latter at the city of Saragassa.

Section A is hazardous but possible during rapid May thaws or after heavy periods of rain. Sections B and C have water releases from the dam so can be paddled **all the year round**.

SECTION A (from Sta. Helena to Biescas)

5 km of Class III+   Kayaking ★   Scenery ★

Put In

At 5 km above Biescas take the small road towards L'Hermita de Sta. Helena to access the Rio Gállego at the road bridge.

Take Out

At Biescas at the road bridge towards Torla to the east.

Description

Apart from some Class III sections where the river splits this is for the most part a straightforward paddle. Barrages upstream of this section severely curtail any paddling opportunities above here.

SECTION B (from Embalse de la Pena to the road bridge)

7 km of Class II-III (4)   Kayaking ★ ★   Scenery ★ ★ ★

Put In

After crossing the lake it is possible to leave vehicles at a right hand bend immediately after the tunnel, access to the water is available below. An alternative is to put in about I km below the water outlet from the 'Barrage de la Pena' via a Class 6 path!.

Take Out

This is at the road bridge on the main road towards the village of **Ayerbe**.

Description

The river flows at the foot of the towering sandstone of the Mallos de Riglos - popular with climbers and para-gliders and this is a grand sight particularly at sunset. This the section is runnable **throughout the year** because of water releases from the dam and this makes it popular with rafting companies.

There are numerous rapids on this run with some narrowed sections between large rocks. When just in sight of the Mallos de Riglos watch out for a rapid with a Class 4 siphon in the middle of the river and a second but lesser example further down between some large rocks. These can be passed to left or right but avoid a swim in this section! The river mellows out for the last 3 km with just Class II rapids.

Section C

5 km of Class II (3)   Kayaking ★   Scenery ★

Put In
As the take our above, at the road bridge, a few km above **Ayerbe**.

Take Out
Above Ayerbe take the road towards the village of **St. Eulalia** de Gállego and take out at the road bridge encountered after a few km.

Description
This is an ideal section for beginner - with warm water in summer and not too demanding rapids. As for the previous section paddling is possible **all year round**.

For the Record
We have paddled the **Rio Sia** which flows south from La Tendenera and the Col de Cotefablo between Biescas and Torla. We put in at the road bridge about 10 km from Biesca towards Torla at the village of Gavin and then ran 7 km of Class II-III (4). We had many portages because of three barrages and fallen trees and so do not recommend this river.

Ben Love worked as a raft guide on the Gállego and writes:

'The village of '**Murillo de Gállego** on route A132 between Jaca and Huesca is taken over by rafting and kayaking. The local bar is called in Spanish 'The Funnel' named after a rapid on the river and is generally open all night with great food and music and full of kayakers and guides from all over the world working or on their way through. It is also popular with climbers and mountain bikers.

The section (mentioned in the text) is known as El Embudo (The Funnel) and is the stretchn on the river about 100 yards long with several of siphons. This stretch was created artificially by the dynamiting of the cliff on the left for a railway tunnel. It should be treated with respect but is out of character with the rest of the river - ask local paddlers for advice.'

Canyon de Lavansa.

Río Urrobi.

Río Urtxuria.

Río Gállego, "parcours classique".

Río Véral sous le soleil espagnol.

Vallée de la haute Noguera Pallaresa.

Río Magdalena.

BASSIN DU RÍO ARA

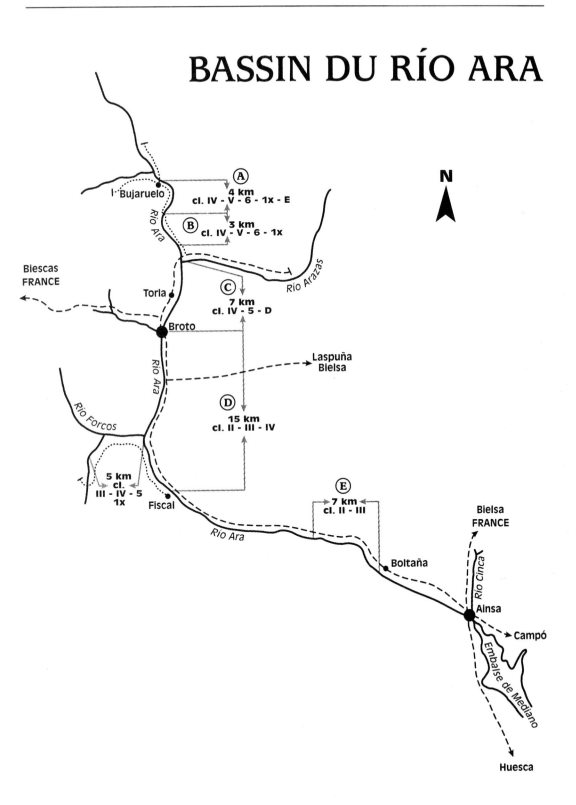

Bassin du Río Ara

Tourist Offices

TORLA
TORISMO
Acceso sur de Torla
Tél : 974 48 61 52

AINSA
TORISMO
Avda. Pirenaica, s/n
Tél : 974 50 07 67

Rafting & Kayak Companies

Aguas Blancas
Avda Sobrarbe 4
22330 Ainsa
Tel : 974 51 00 08
www.pirineo.com/aguasblancas

EKM Adventure Sports Center
Avenida de Prdesa 26
22330Ainsa
Tel : 670 369 091, Fax: 974 510 090
www.ekm.es

Saratillo
Avenida Pirnaica 11
22330 Ainsa
Tel : 974 50 07 25
www.pireneo.com/sarratillo24

Río Ara

The River

The Rio Ara offers you more than 40 km paddling grouped into sections with different classes of difficulty. Only one dam on the lower part, 8 km above Boltana, hampers our paddling freedom. This is one of the **great classic Pyrenean rivers.**

Its source is behind the rocky amphitheatre of Gavarnie beneath Vignemale. These two locations have numerous summits greater than 3000 m. It is fed mainly, therefore from melt water and can be paddled from May to June and often into July in the right snow conditions. The steep section B is often viable after warm weather in March.

Water levels

For your information these are our estimates of water levels based on the gauge at **Torla** - see below:

        80 to 110 is low enough to allow paddling on sections A and B with confidence.

        110 to 150 at this higher level sections A and B are still feasible but section C

        needs to be scouted fully.

Above that we advise against doing sections A and B. Section C remains feasible, even with more water, but two passages must be rated 5 almost 6. In big water sections D and E don't pose any particular problems but you must remain vigilant.

SECTION A (from Bujaruelo)
4 km of class IV-V (5+) (x) E   Kayaking ★★★   Scenery ★★★

Put In
Drive up the valley of the rio Ara by taking a track that leaves on the left just after the road bridge of Los Navarros about 3 km upstream from the village of **Torla**. This section is the highest we know. The put in is at the end of the official car track at the camp site of Bujaruelo.

Take Out
This is at the only foot bridge between the camp site of Bujaruelo and the road bridge of Los Navarros.

Description
The first kilometre is rather quiet before you get to the first portage that sets the scene for the rest of the descent. The river becomes canyon-like with pronounced technical rapids. The class 6 hazard is a large drop to the right of a huge rock. It can be portaged on the left bank.

SECTION B ('les dalles')
3 km of class IV-V (6) (x)   Kayaking ★★★   Scenery ★★★

Put In
At the take out as above - at the only foot bridge between the road bridge of Los Navarros and the camp site of Bujaruelo about 3.5 km above the Los Navarros bridge.

Take Out
Take out must be made about 400 m upstream from the bridge at Los Navarros. Some 20 m after the wooden gates a footpath comes down to the river. We advise you to check and inspect this take out before putting on. It is absolutely essential to take out on the left bank before the river enters the next gorge.

Description

This is **marvellous run** from every point of view - in terms of the paddling, the rapids, and the landscape!

The first bit of the run is class IV and a good warm up - technical, between large rocks and without great difficulty. This leads to an impassable drop which should be portaged on the left bank on the track and then the first class 6 rapid which is best portaged on the right bank - you can inspect this before putting back in from the path just below the concrete ramp.

What then follows is a succession of slides, some big, some small but none especially noteworthy, and all pass rapidly by. Taking a turn to the left you come across the second class 6 rapid that can be viewed from the right bank. This is a slide of about 30 m and best **not** taken on the right.

There are more very nice rapids before you have to start to think about getting out on the left bank about 400 m upstream from the road bridge at Los Navarros.

SECTION C   (from the bridge of Los Navarros to Broto)

7 km of class IV (5) D   Kayaking ★★★   Scenery ★★

Put In

This is downstream of road bridge of Los Navarros, 2.5 km above Torla. At the bridge take the foot path going downstream on the left bank that leads to the river just at the end of the gorges. On your drive up the valley we recommend that you stop to inspect the **weir at Torla** and to check the water gauge.

Take Out

Take out is easy at the village of **Broto**

Description

This descent is less steep than the previous one but is still interesting. It is a popular for commercial rafting. The pronounced rapids are technical or big depending on the water level, but on the whole are feasible because they are interspersed with good pools and quiet stretches in which to recover.

At the village of **Torla** there is a very attractive stone bridge immediately followed by a **nasty weir** that is usually portaged on the left bank to scout and see if the weir is runnable. There is a **water gauge** here.

Immediately after putting back on the water, ferry to the right to enter the next gorge section - a fine finish to this section.

SECTION D (from Broto to Fiscal)

15 km of class II-III-IV   Kayaking ★★   Scenery ★★

Put In

At the village of Broto

Take Out

At the village of Fiscal

Description

The river widens and flows over gravel beds. Rapids are big and class II-III for the first half of the run then after the confluence with the Forcos the rapids are still big and definitely a more powerful class III+ or IV. In high water this becomes a big bouncy run with large waves and holes but nothing too spectacular.

SECTION E (Gorges de Boltana)

7 km of class II-III   Kayaking ★ ★   Scenery ★ ★

Put In

At the large dam at the entrance to the gorge about 8 km above Boltana. From the road take the foot path that leads to the dam. There is a water outlet pipe about 5 m downstream from the dam.

Take Out

About 1.5 km upstream from the village of Boltana below the road bridge leading to Sabinanigo.

Description

This is a very attractive section through beautiful gorges with no particular difficulty. At the time of writing the dam is not in operation - we suggest that you enquire locally from rafting companies in Ainsa for information about water releases.

Río Forcos

5 km of class III-IV (5) (x)   Kayaking ★ ★   Scenery ★ ★

The River

The rio Forcas is a tributary of the right bank of the rio Ara, having its source in low level mountains so snow melt is unreliable - but on the other hand you can always find water to paddle after heavy rain.

Put In

At the village of **Fiscal** take the road to the right after the bridge then the track going up on the left. Continue on this track until about 2 km after the village of **Bergua** you approach the river where there is an imposing electricity pylon. The put in is here, cutting through the fields to get to the river. For your information, once past Bergau the track is not in very good condition!

Take Out

To take out its better to carry on down the river Ara and take out at the village of **Fiscal**.

Description

The river is small and technical. The portage is in the first third of the descent and a little way after this a large tributary flows into the river on the left. The following section is steeper with a few drops of 3 to 4m.

We advise you to look at the water level on your drive up the valley and before putting in. About 5 km up valley from **Fiscal** is a large electricity transformer at the edge of the road - here you are at the same level as the confluence of the Forcos and the Ara. If there isn't much water in the river but it still looks paddleable then we advise putting in just above the village of Bergua by going along a foot path that rejoins the river at the confluence with the tributary coming in on the left.

Río Forcos.

Bassin du Río Cinca

Tourist Offices

BIELSA
TORISMO
Ctra. Parzán, s/n
Tel : 974 50 10 00

AINSA
TORISMO
Avda. Pirenaica, s/n
Tél : 974 50 07 67

PLAN
TORISMO
Ayuntamiento
Tél : 974 50 06 01

Rafting & Kayak Companies

Aguas Blancas
Avda Sobrarbe 4
22330 Ainsa
Tel : 974 51 00 08
www.pirineo.com/aguasblancas

EKM Adventure Sports Center
Avenida de Prdesa 26
22330 Ainsa
Tel : 670 369 091, Fax: 974 510 090
www.ekm.es

Saratillo
Avenida Pirnaica 11
22330 Ainsa
Tel : 34 974 50 07 25
www.pireneo.com/sarratillo24

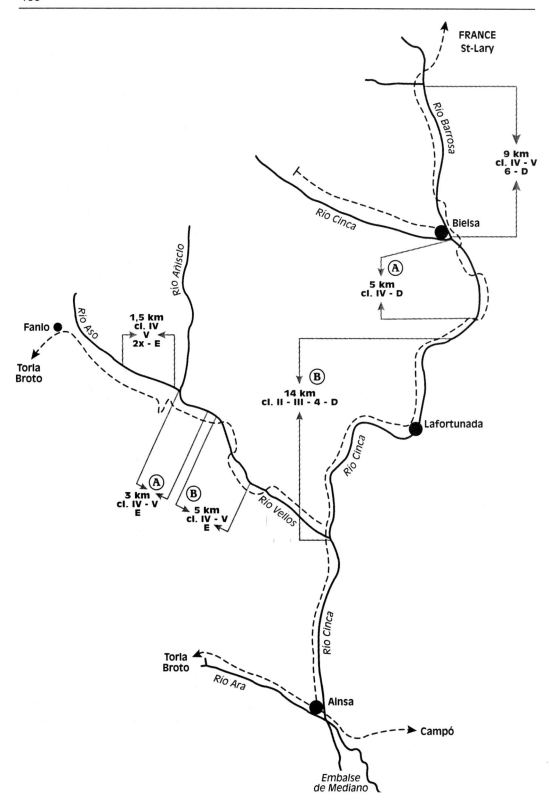

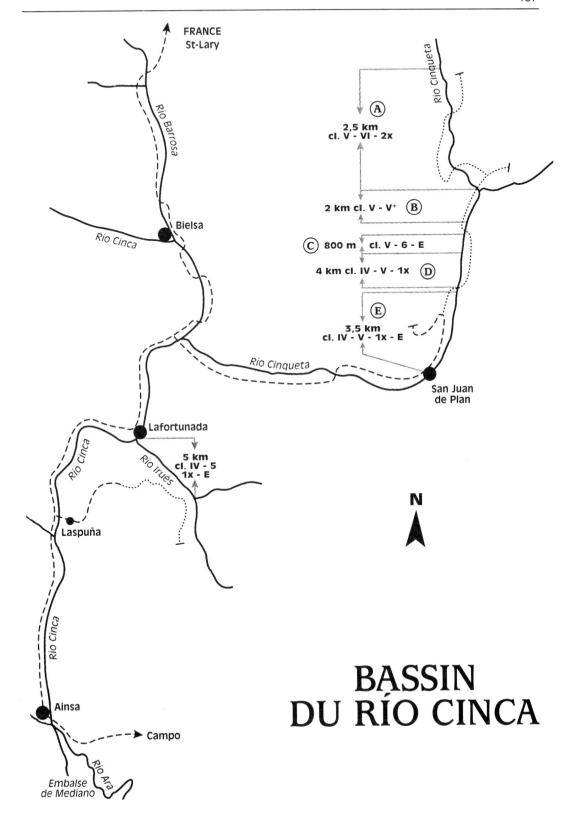

FRANCE
St-Lary

Río Barrosa

Río Cinca

Bielsa

Río Cinqueta

(A)

2,5 km
cl. V - VI - 2x

2 km cl. V - V⁺ (B)

(C) 800 m cl. V - 6 - E

4 km cl. IV - V - 1x (D)

(E)

3,5 km
cl. IV - V - 1x - E

Río Cinqueta

San Juan
de Plan

Lafortunada

5 km
cl. IV - 5
1x - E

Río Cinca

Río Irués

Laspuña

N

Río Cinca

Ainsa

Campo

Río Ara

Embalse
de Mediano

BASSIN
DU RÍO CINCA

Río Cinca

The River

The Rio Cinca is fed by Monte Perdido 3355m and surrounding peaks and it has its source in the majestic Circo de Pineto. It has a wide river bed and abundant melt water but because of the numerous dams and water extraction points paddling is limited and is at its best in the month of May thanks to the thaw.

SECTION A (from Bielsa)

5km of class IV D   Kayaking ★ ★   Scenery ★ ★

Put In

At the village of Bielsa at the confluence of the Cinca and the Barrosa

Take Out

About 4.5 km downstream from Bielsa at the road bridge before the river drops into a huge impassable chaos.

Description

The river is broad with big, technical rapids that are not too difficult. This section is still good at high water levels but be careful not to paddle past the take out point as the chaos is not exactly tempting!

SECTION B

14 km of class II-III (4) D   Kayaking ★ ★   Scenery ★ ★

Put in

At the confluence of the Cinqueta and the Cinca.

Take Out

At the confluence of the Vellos and the Cinca.

Description

This section is pleasant and varied. At the beginning the descent is through a canyon and the pronounced rapids are class III (4). Then the rock faces draw back and you reach the dam of Laspuna in the village of **Lafortunada**. Get out on the right bank to portage the dam, putting back in immediately after. The run below here has more fine rapids but also some bends where the current sweeps you against undercut banks.

Río Cinqueta

The River

A mountain chain with peaks higher than 3000 m (among them the Posets massif) feeds most of this river so the thaw usually lasts for the months of May and June and is a free flowing river with not a single weir to disrupt the wildlife or wild paddling.

Water levels:

50 m downstream of the first road bridge (the put in for Section A) is a small house on the edge of the water with a water gauge. There are two gauges, we refer to the one level with the small house on the right bank.

> 75 on the scale seems to us the maximum level for the 'les Gorges Rouges'- Section C.
>
> 100 to 110 is the optimum level for the high section - Section B.
>
> 100 to 140 allows for calm paddling on the classic section - Section D.
>
> 100 to 145 is a good level to fully appreciate the lower part. Also if there is plenty of
>
> water in these sections, it may be good chance to run the upper Cinqueta (section A).

SECTION A (high)

2.5 km of class V-VI (xx)   Kayaking ★★★   Scenery ★★★

Put In

After the village of **San Juan de Plan** take the track that goes straight on then bends to the left to go back up the valley. On this track you will pass the first foot bridge (the road crosses from the right to the left bank) and 50 m downstream is the **water gauge** referred to above. Then some km further on there is a second foot bridge (with the river canyon below) and you carry on for about 3 km. The track cuts into the river again and this is the take out point. Further on the track splits into two, take the left one. There is another foot bridge 800 m above and 500 m further the track ends. The put in is below the little foot bridge at the end of the track.

Take Out

This is described above

Description

The first 500 m present no real difficulty except for the rapid under the foot bridge where you put in. A little further on the gradient becomes steeper and you reach the first portage (on the right bank). The follows stretch is very continuous until you arrive at a large chute visible from the foot bridge. Then the river calms down a little for about 600 m before reaching a beautiful chute of about 7 m, quickly followed by a second portage made on the left bank.

SECTION B (upper)

2 km of class V-V+   Kayaking ★★   Scenery ★★★

Put In

At the take out for the previous section - about 2.5 km above the second foot bridge. The river runs through fields and is bordered by the track.

Take Out

Driving up the valley the take out can be spotted about 200 m upstream from the second foot bridge. You can seize the opportunity to inspect the powerful drop of about 4 m followed by a whitish narrow pass which are the last hazards before taking out on the right bank.

Description

The rapids present you with pronounced ledges, attractive slides, lovely chutes and beautiful very deep drops. In high water levels we recommend that you carefully scout all of the rapids and drops before putting on - particularly one 6m chute that must be shot on the left.

SECTION C ('les Gorges rouges')

800 m of class V (6) E   Kayaking ★★★   Scenery ★★★

Put In

The put in is below the second foot bridge going back up the valley. You have to go down into the woods about 500 m downstream of this bridge, on the left bank.

Take Out

The take out is about 1 km downstream from the foot bridge of the put in point - taking a path that goes down the left bank and leads to another foot bridge. The start of this path is on a right hand bend.

Description

From the beginning you enter into the spirit of things with a chute that can be portaged on the right bank. It is vital to not to attempt these gorges at too high a water level as this chute cannot then be carried and develops a strong 'keeper'. We reckon 75 on the water gauge is the maximum (see above).

SECTION D ('classic')

4 km of class IV-V (x)   Kayaking ★★★   Scenery ★★★

Put In - at the take out of the previous section.

Take Out

Some 100 m downstream from the first foot bridge near the small house with a foot bridge and water gauge.

Description

This classic section is **one of the most beautiful descents in the Pyrenees**, due as much to the sumptuous setting as the diversity and difficulty of the rapids you come across. We say no more!

SECTION E (lower)

3.5 km of class IV-V (x) E   Kayaking ★★★   Scenery ★★

Put In

Near to the small house mentioned in the take out of the previous section. But it is best to go along the field on the right and put in about 100 m downstream so as to avoid a bad drop where bank support is difficult.

Take Out-

In the village of **San Juan de Plan** - take the road on the right leading to the river.

Description

This section is canyon-like, narrow and very technical. The portage occurs after about 1 km when the river becomes like a canyon - it is imperative to take out on the left bank and to carry your kayak for 150 m to put in again immediately after the chute. The portage takes you around two chutes, the first of which is very vicious with no chance of bank support.

The rest of the descent is very varied and enjoyable - worthy of lingering over, both at the time and afterwards in the bar.

Vallée du rio Vellos.

Río Aso

1.5 km of class IV-V (xx) E   Kayaking ★★   Scenery ★★

The River

The Rio Aso is a small river that joins the Rio Anisclo to form the Rio Vellos which then flows into the Cinca upstream of Ainsa. It rises in a scenic area of limestone hills just to the south of the Parque National de Ordesa. Although principally relying on rainfall the river can be paddled after the early May thaw or earlier if in a warm period.

Note that the Rio Aso is itself outside the National Park and can therefore be paddled freely in contrast to Rio Anisclo and Rio Vellos.

Put In

Drive up the valley of the Rio Vellos to the confluence of the rios Aso and Anisclo. Stop here to check the water level at the take out. Then follow the road for a further 2 km until you cross a dry ravine. Leave the car here and take the path on the left of the ravine to access the river.

Take Out

This is at the confluence - the parking area is on a pronounced left hand bend as you drive up the road.
On the river, take out after about 1.5 km and before an absolutely impassable drop of about a dozen metres. From river right the path leads up to the parking area. (From this parking area several beautiful trails lead up into the National Park and the Valle de Anisclo).

Description

The volume of water increases progressively along this section due to many side streams and it is therefore important that the water level at the put in is not too high. If you scrape a bit initially then the level is probably ok - but it is better to double check first by also looking closely at the level at the take out.

The nature of this run is well-marked drops interspersed with pools.

Río Vellos

For the Record

The Rio Vellos is now part of the National Park and unfortunately all forms of paddling are **strictly forbidden**. The Vellos is a very special river running in a tight, narrow and committing gorge throughout. A short stretch of the lower river is outside the park boundary but this has a waterfall that cannot be shot and cannot be portaged! For the curious, there is a path along the river from the first road bridge up the valley from which you can view the latter.

Río Barrosa

9 km of class IV-V (6) D   Kayaking ★ ★ ★   Scenery ★ ★

The River
The Rio Barrosa is a small left bank tributary of the Rio Cinca that joins it at **Bielsa**. The catchment is restricted and there is only a small chance of finding enough water - this is not helped by a water intake above the put in that removes most of the water. The best chance is during May or after heavy rain.

Put In
After crossing into Spain via the Bielsa Tunnel the river is found after a series of sharp bends. Put in on the right bank about 100 m downstream of the road bridge.

Take Out - At the village of **Bielsa** at the confluence of the Rio Barrosa and Rio Cinca.

Description
The first 200 m contain everything the canoeist can possibly meet - narrows, sills, drops, falls, linked rapids etc. and indeed may not be practicable at high water level. The remainder of the section is somewhat more restrained but enjoyable. The Barrosa hydro-electric station at 3 km must be portaged on the left.

If you wish the paddle can be extended into the Rio Cinca (see that description).

Río Irues

5 km of class IV (5) (x) E   Kayaking ★ ★ ★   Scenery ★ ★ ★

The River
Although the catchment is feeble at least this river does not suffer from water abstraction and there is the chance of a paddle during the May thaw. The special blue colour of the river gives Rio Azul as an alternative name!

Put In
The put in is a tricky 15 minute journey by road and a further 40 minute descent on a track:

About 8 km downstream of Lafortunada towards Ainsa, take the left turn to **Laspuna** and here turn left after the combined bar and village store. A bit further on at 200 m past the cemetery take a road and then at 2.2 km a track which run south-north to reach the Irues valley. 10.5 km from the cemetery one can see from the road the confluence with the Barranco de La Garona, which is the put in. Leave the vehicles here and descend on foot by a small track to a house and a field and then by a path to the left to bring you to this confluence after a further 200 m.

Alternatively, to avoid this long and awkward shuttle you can carry the kayaks up the valley setting out from near the church in **Lafortunada** via a path to arrive at the confluence above in about an hour.

Take Out - at the barrage de Laspuna at Lafortunada.

Description
Taking into account the lengthy shuttle it is best to evaluate the water level first by looking at the river at the take out near the barrage. This river is in a wild setting, remote from the road and a trip is wonderful and well worth the effort. Do not attempt in high water.

Río Irues.

BASSIN
DU RÍO ESERA

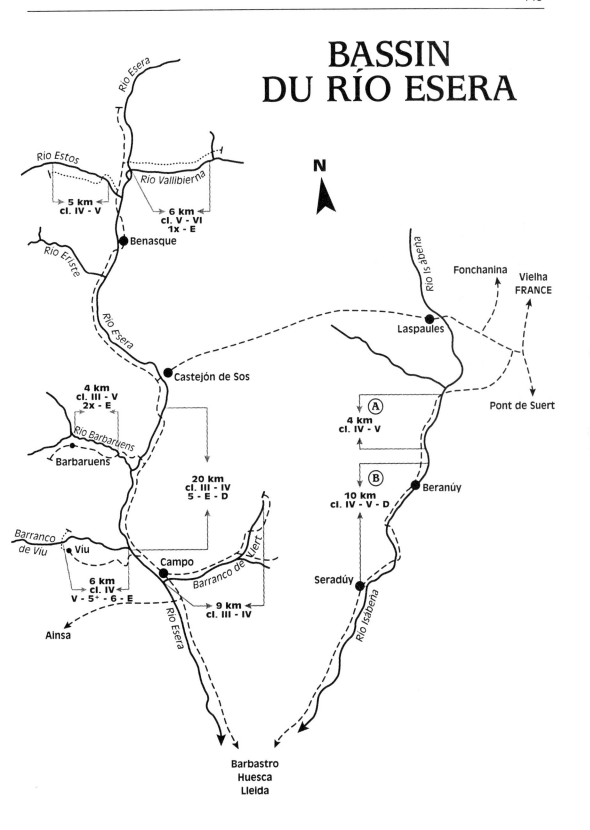

N

Río Esera

Río Estos

Río Vallibierna

5 km
cl. IV - V

6 km
cl. V - VI
1x - E

● Benasque

Río Eriste

Río Is ábeña

Fonchanina

Vielha
FRANCE

Río Esera

Laspaules ●

● Castejón de Sos

Pont de Suert

4 km
cl. III - V
2x - E

Ⓐ

4 km
cl. IV - V

Río Barbaruens

● Barbaruens

20 km
cl. III - IV
5 - E - D

Ⓑ

10 km
cl. IV - V - D

● Beranúy

Barranco
de Viu

● Víu

Barranco de Vuert

● Campo

Seradúy ●

6 km
cl. IV
V - 5⁺ - 6 - E

9 km
cl. III - IV

Ainsa

Río Esera

Río Isábeña

Barbastro
Huesca
Lleida

Bassin du Río Esera

Tourist Offices

Rafting & Kayak Companies

Benasque
TORISMO
Tel: 974 55 12 89

Casteon de Sos
TORISMO
Tel: 974 55 30 00

Aguas Blancas
Avda Sobrarbe 4
22330 Ainsa
Tel : 974 51 00 08
www.pirineo.com/aguasblancas

It was a tough looking rapid, and everything was in the
wrong place today thought Nigel, himself included ....

Río Esera

20 km of class III-IV (5) E D   Kayaking ★ ★   Scenery ★ ★

The River
With its source under the peaks of the Massif des Posets (3371 m) and Massif l'Aneto (3408 m) the Rio Esera is one of the most important rivers of the Pyrenees. Unfortunately the many barrages on the river and its tributaries limit paddling possibilities to the thaw periods in May and early June.

Put In
This is downstream of the village of **Castejon de Sos** on the N 260 .

Take Out - At the barrage of **Campo** near the N 260.

Description
Certainly meriting a detour this picturesque but narrow run can be reconnoitred throughout from the N 260. The class 5 rapid involves an ugly looking rock ledge in the early part of the gorge section and where it is difficult to take adequate safety measures. A second difficult section occurs about 500 m before the barrage.

In high water it is difficult to stop or break out in the gorge sections.

Río Vallibierna

6.5 km of class V-VI (x) E   Kayaking ★ ★ ★   Scenery ★ ★

The River
From a source near the 3000 m mountain from which it takes its name the Rio Vallibierna becomes a left bank tributary of the Rio Esera. The constrained nature of the river only allows paddling at the beginning and end of thaw periods - the latter in late **June to early July**.

Put In
High up the Esera valley go through **Benasque** to the lake section and just past this take the track to the right. Cross the Esera and then go past the campsite and take the track into the valley of the Valibierna to the Put In about 8.5 km further on where a tributary enters from the right. There is no difficulty with access here from the track.

Take Out - at the lake on the Esera.

Description
This is one of the **most difficult rivers of the Pyrenees**. The gradient averages 100 m/km and in some places is more sustained - so there are many drops and waterfall on this run. The largest fall (more than 15 m) occurs just after a footbridge about 2.5 km after the put in. Added to this are many chutes, like toboggan runs, some up to 15 m, and several serious rapids that demand great attention and technical expertise.   A strong, organised, expert, but small team is essential.

About half way, in the midst of a rocky section, a portage must be made around an ugly looking ledge.

Note importantly that the bed can shift from one year to another and also that **trees** can be carried into the river as a result of avalanches.

Do not attempt in too high a water - 3-4 cumecs seems about right.

Río Estos

5 km of class IV-V   Kayaking ★★★   Scenery ★★★

The River
Like the previous river this is also a right bank tributary of the Rio Esero, entering the latter above **Benasque**. East of the Massif des Posets the river draws water from a range of 3000 m summits and can be viable throughout the thaw. There are no barrages on this run to hinder paddling.

Put In
Take the track (suitable only for 4X4 vehicles) to the left 3 km above Benasque towards the Refuge d'Estos. (when this track is impassable then the alternative is a 2 hour carry) to the Barranco de Montidiego and then follow a path to the right along the Barranco down to the river below the Turmo waterfalls.

Take Out - At the barrage seen on the way up the valley.

Description
Set amidst wild beautiful scenery the river is best considered in three parts.

From the start to the small bridge leading to the Santa Ana maisonette the river is Class IV-V with one 5+ rapid in the middle of a gorge section.

This is followed by an easier Class II-III section down to the bridge carrying a track over the river and this allows some respite and a chance to admire the scenery.

From here is the final and most demanding Class V section caused by a gradient of 110 m/km !

For the Record
We have also tried the Rio Eriste, a right bank tributary of the Esero about 4 km downstream of Benasque. Go up a valley by the track suitable for vehicles to put in when the latter passes the right bank and where various streams converge to form the Eriste. We only managed the first 300 m before a big drop stopped further progress.

Note also in the lower section of the Eriste valley there is a superb waterfall on the right bank.

Barranco de Viú

6 km of class IV-V (5+) (6) E   Kayaking ★★   Scenery ★★

The River
The Rio de Viú is a right bank tributary of the Esera entering the lake formed by the Cambo barrage. Although mainly dependent on rainfall it might still be possible to paddle during a heavy thaw in late April or early May.

Put In
From **Campo** go up the valley take the left turn at the barrage. This leads to the village of **Viú** after which take the track down to the river which here is rather small.

Take Out -
At the lake above the Campo barrage where there is adequate parking.

Description

The main flow (approx. 80%) is created from water entering from the right about 1 km below the put in described. Down to this point there is little of interest but note the 3 m drop passed on the way which is best portaged on the left.

Below this first section there are some good rapids with the class 6 fall just after a substantial footbridge. Portage this to the left to re-enter after the gorge.

Danger - note that the lake at the barrage has a water intake which is entirely unprotected. Getting sucked down this vortex could make an interesting but fatal climax to any kayak trip.

To assess the flow in the Viú look at the stretch before the river discharges into the lake.

Río Barbaruens

4 km of class IV-V (xx) E   Kayaking ★★   Scenery ★★★

The River

The Rio Barbaruens is a right bank estuary of the Esera rising under summits of 2500-3000 m. The thaw, generally up around mid May, can be inadequate and you may have to rely on additional rain.

Put In

About 15 km above **Campo** take the left turn from the N 260 at **Seira** in the direction of the village of **Barbaruens**. Leave the vehicle about 2 km above the only road bridge and take the track to the right to cross the river by a footbridge after perhaps 30 minutes of portage. At low water the drop beneath the bridge is probable shootable, if not put in 300 m lower down on the right within the wood.

Take out

At the road bridge mentioned earlier or carry on down a Class II section to where the river joins the Esera .

Description

When there is sufficient water this is a fine committing run with canyon like sections, beautiful ledge drops and toboggan chutes.

Barranco de Llert

9 km of class III-IV   Kayaking ★   Scenery ★★

The River

The Barranco de Llert is a left bank tributary of the Esera, entering the latter at **Campo**. The moderate summits of the catchment gives adequate water only after heavy rain or better still if the rain helps out during the thaw period. Only attempt when plenty of water is available.

Put In

From Campo head off in the direction of Villas del Turbon and at 6 km take the left turn to put in at the confluence of two streams just before the village of **Llert**.

Take Out - On the C 139 just downstream of Campo.

Description

The first 4 km are technical and reach class IV. After this the river widens and becomes class III.

Río Vallibierna.

Río Isabeña

The River
This left bank tributary of the Esera is found at its best in early May.

SECTION A (upper)
4 km of class IV-V   Kayaking ★★   Scenery ★★

Put In
From the N 260 between Castejon de Sos and Pont de Suert take the road through **Bonansa** and after the Alto de Bonansa descend to the Rio Isabena. Keep going to embark at the confluence with the Rio Blanco (on some maps called the Rio Espes).

Take Out
Before the gorges 4 km downstream.

Description
This section is technical with well defined drops but unfortunately often blocked or impassable. From what we could see from the road the gorges section below appears impassable.

For the Record
The section above this has been examined by us but the difficult narrow rocky passage did not seem worth attempting.

SECTION B (Monastere to Seraduy)
10 km of class IV-V D   Kayaking ★★   Scenery ★★

Put In
From **Bonansa** the put in is after the gorge section and below the bridge which leads to the Monastere de Obarra.

Take Out
On the right bank on leaving **Serraduy**.

Description
This run is only viable when the water is high and then there are rapids approaching Class V.

In the first quarter of the run you will be surprised by a large double ledge hidden by a bend in the river and where steep rock faces then leave little room to manoeuvre! Further on down, a dam which is visible from the road which can normally be shot.

Bassin du Río Noguera Ribagorçana

Tourist Offices

www.ribagorca.com

EL PONT DE SUERT (25700)
TORISMO
Plaza del Mercadal, 7
Tel : 973 69 00 05

VIELLA (525530)
TORISMO
Avda Castièro, 15
Tel : 973 64 09 79

Rafting & Kayak Companies

Nosueza Aventure
Ciutat de Lleida
25520 El Pont de Suert
Tel : 973 69 00 55,
Fax: 973 69 01 55

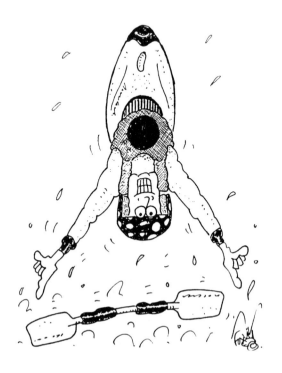

BASSIN DU RÍO NOGUERA RIBAGORÇANA

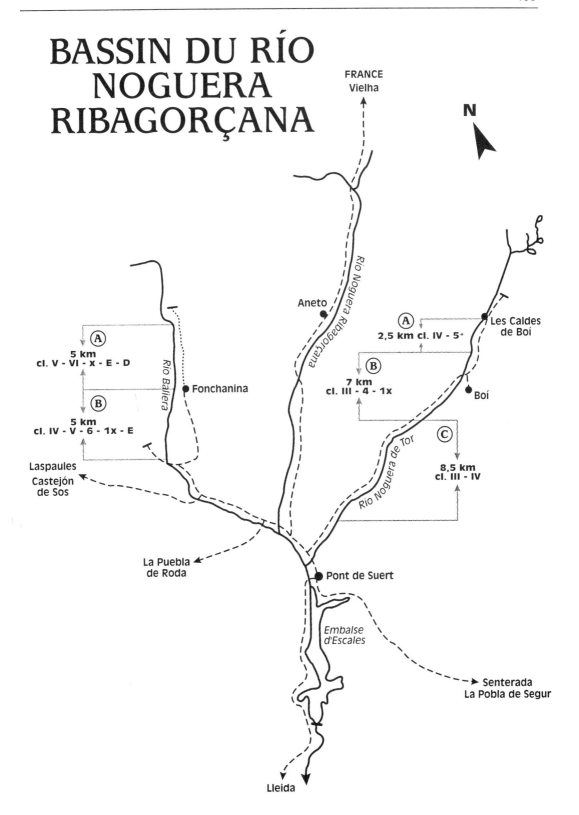

FRANCE
Vielha

N

Aneto

Río Noguera Ribagorçana

Río Baliera

A
5 km
cl. V - VI - x - E - D

B
5 km
cl. IV - V - 6 - 1x - E

Fonchanina

Laspaules
Castejón
de Sos

La Puebla
de Roda

A
2,5 km cl. IV - 5⁺

Les Caldes
de Boí

B
7 km
cl. III - 4 - 1x

Boí

C
8,5 km
cl. III - IV

Río Noguera de Tor

Pont de Suert

Embalse
d'Escales

Senterada
La Pobla de Segur

Lleida

Río Baliera "Parcours A".

Río Baliera

The River

Set in a deep valley, the Rio Baliera, is a tributary of the Rio Ribagorçana. It relies on thaw and rain for supply but the thaw may pass unnoticed further down as water abstraction is made direct into the Ribagorçana.

The water level can be assessed from the scale at the road bridge towards the village of **Ribeira**. A reading of 40 cm represents a good level for above and below the water intake.

SECTION A

5 km of class V-VI (xx) E D   Kayaking ★   Scenery ★★

Put In

Go up the road along the left bank through the villages of Ardanuy, Castanesa and finally **Fonchanina**. Here the road ends and you continue along a track for 3-4 km to some isolated houses. Access is gained from the track just downstream of these houses.

Take Out

If you do not wish to continue down section B then leave a car in **Fonchanina** and take out here. The path to the village leads off from a solid footbridge - on the river this is after the second big portage around a large drop leading to a narrow passage.

Description

Until the water abstraction point at about one third of the run the valley is pleasantly open with agreeable paddling although there are some tricky bits to overcome. Stop 200 m above the dam and water abstraction point to portage and re-enter at the footbridge some 300 m below it.

The stretch that follows is well worthwhile but requires a strong team as the road is at some distance and several difficult portages are necessary - there are some narrow gorge sections which are very difficult and committing!

SECTION B

5 km of class IV-V (6) (x) E   Kayaking ★★   Scenery ★★

Put In

At **Fonchanina,** the take out of the previous section, see above.

Take Out

At the road bridge some 100 m upstream of where the road forks to Ribeira and Ardanuy.

Description

This section is slightly less exhausting than that above and merits an attempt. The rapids and drops are well defined and the whole run is in a stupendous setting.

Río Noguera de Tor

The River

The Noguera de Tor flows into the Noguera Ribagorçana some 2 km upstream of **Pont de Suert**. With a catchment fed by thaw from the Massif d'Aigues Tortes (up to 3000 m) the early section is spoilt by the barrage upstream of Caldès.de Boy. The river is magnificent but water releases from the barrage can make water levels very variable (and potentially hazardous).

SECTION A (upper)

2.5 km of class IV (5+)   Kayaking ★★   Scenery ★★

Put In

At the start of **Caldès.de Boy**

Take Out

At the hydro-electric station of Caldès.2.5 km downstream of the put in.

Description

A very steep run with one 5 m, and a toboggan chute of 10 m that add even more interest to an exciting descent. The river was very encumbered, tight and rocky, when we did our descent with only 20 cm on the gauge at Caldès..

SECTION B (middle)

7 km of class III (4) (x)   Kayaking ★★   Scenery ★★

Put In

Below the hyrdo station at Caldès..

Take Out

At the barrage at **Barruera**, 7 km downstream.

Description

As noted earlier we did this trip at low water. Watch out for a big drop of 7-8 m which must be portaged - and beware the large siphon here under a huge block on the left. This portage is via river right but may be difficult in high water. Take care to look out for the approach to this chute!

SECTION C (lower)

8.5 km of class III-IV   Kayaking ★★   Scenery ★★

Put In

Below the barrage at Barruera, the take out for the preceding section.

Take Out

At the barrage at **Llesp** some 8.5 km further downstream.

Description

A lively but not too demanding section with which to complete the whole trip.

(Because of low water we did not complete the section to the Noguera Ribagorçana but from what we could see this looked like it was Class III for the 5 km or so to the confluence).

Bassin du Río Noguera Pallaresa

Tourist Offices

Esterri d'Aneu
El Albergue Pirinenc
C/Major no.2
Esterri d'Aneu
Lleida
Fax: 973 62 62 11
Tel: 973 62 65 13

Sort
TORISMO
Tel: 973 62 10 02

La Pobla de Segur (25500)
TORISMO
Avgda Veraguer 35
Tel : 973 68 02 57

Rafting & Kayak Companies

Promotur Pallars
Cellers
Tel : 973 25 22 09

Roc Roi
Placa Nostra Sra. De Biuse 8
25595 Llavorsi
Lleida
Tel: 973 62 20 35
Fax : 973 62 21 08
www.rocroi.com

Beni Tours
Tremp
Tel : 973 65 00 31

Río Noguera Pallaresa "Parcours D".

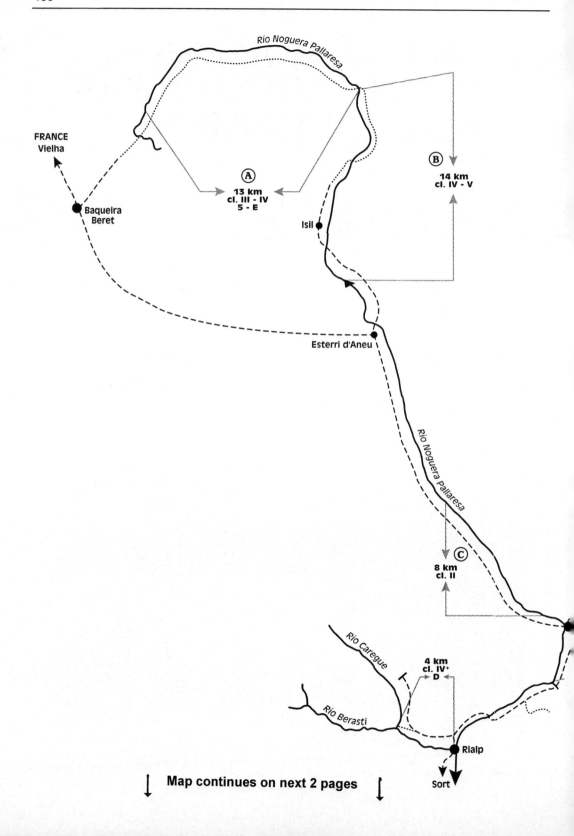

Río Noguera Pallaresa

FRANCE
Vielha

Ⓐ
**13 km
cl. III - IV
5 - E**

Ⓑ
**14 km
cl. IV - V**

● Baqueira
Beret

Isil ●

● Esterri d'Aneu

Río Noguera Pallaresa

Ⓒ
**8 km
cl. II**

Río Caregue

**4 km
cl. IV⁺
D**

Río Berasti

● Rialp

↓ **Map continues on next 2 pages** ↓

Sort

BASSIN DU RÍO NOGUERA PALLARESA

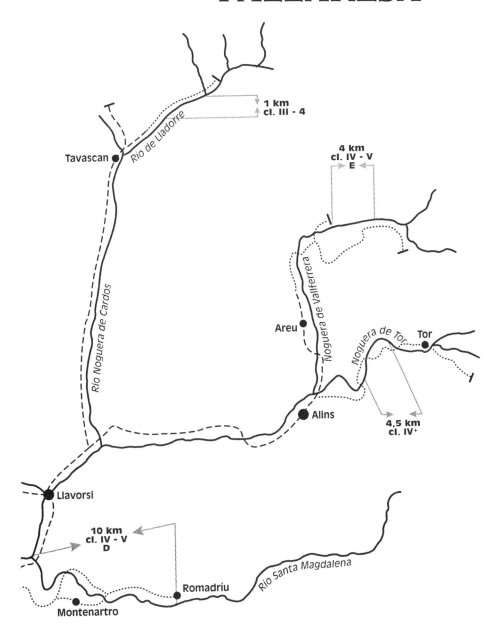

N

1 km
cl. III - 4

4 km
cl. IV - V
E

Tavascan

Río de Lladorre

Río Noguera de Cardos

Noguera de Vallferrera

Areu

Noguera de Tor

Tor

Alins

4,5 km
cl. IV+

Llavorsi

10 km
cl. IV - V
D

Romadríu

Río Santa Magdalena

Montenartro

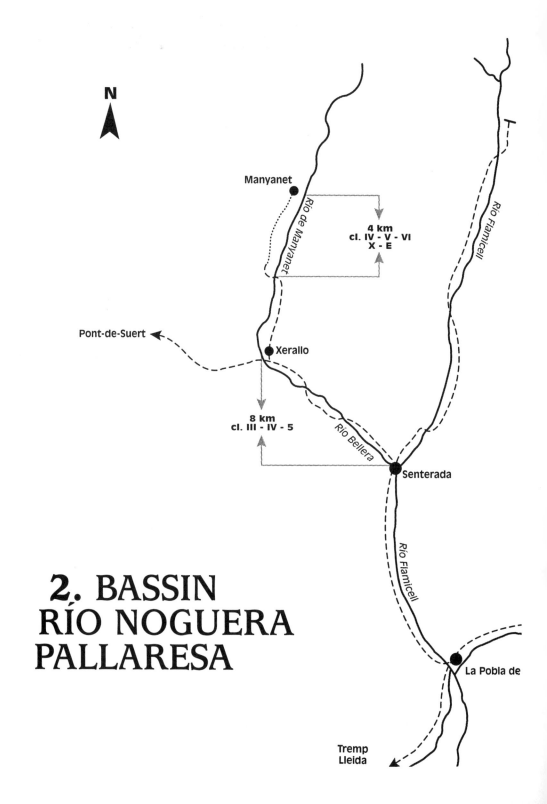

N

Manyanet

Río de Manyanet

4 km
cl. IV - V - VI
X - E

Pont-de-Suert

Xerallo

Río Flamicell

8 km
cl. III - IV - 5

Río Bellera

Senterada

Río Flamicell

2. BASSIN
RÍO NOGUERA
PALLARESA

La Pobla de

Tremp
Lleida

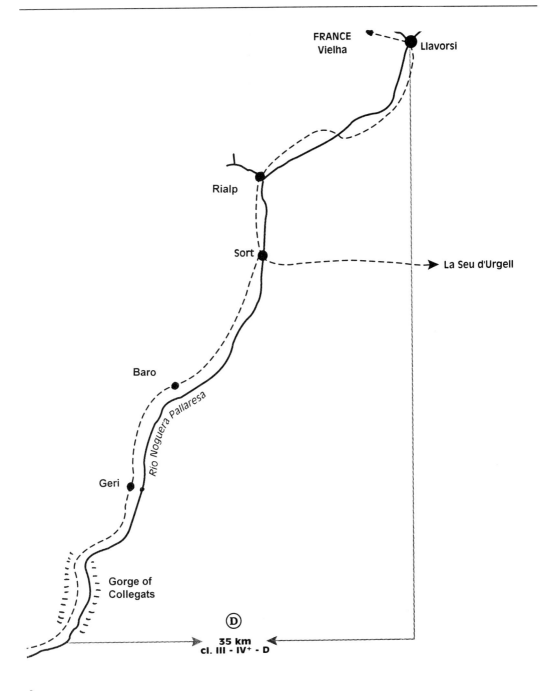

FRANCE
Vielha

Llavorsi

Rialp

Sort

La Seu d'Urgell

Baro

Rio Noguera Pallaresa

Geri

Gorge of
Collegats

Ⓓ

35 km
cl. III - IV⁺ - D

Segur

Río Noguera Pallaresa

The River

The Noguera Pallaresa is without doubt the **largest river in the Pyrenees** and of great interest to paddlers. It has an extensive river basin of wide valleys and is dominated by high mountain peaks so the river is fed by both rainfall and snow melt water. However in contrast to most Spanish rivers the thaw lasts for nearly two months. Also, a large dam downstream from Esterri d'Aneu releases water so this means that you can paddle the lower river practically **all the year round**.

SECTION A (High)

13 km class III-IV (5) E   Kayaking ★★   Scenery ★★★

Put in

Arriving from France, the easiest place to get afloat on this section is through the village of Baqueira Beret and turning left in the direction of Pla de Beret. The put in is about 1 km downstream down a path on the right bank.

From the Spanish side, take the road **Esterri d'Aneu** in the direction of **Boren**, Alos d'Isil. After this village the road becomes a track (usually in good condition) and follow it for about 28km to Pla de Beret (about 1 hour's driving).

Take out

Take out by the first foot bridge downstream of Pla de Beret (about 13.5 km). Going upstream, this foot bridge is where the track crosses from the left to the right bank - the third after the dam at Boren.

Description

This run starts near the source where the Noguera Pallaresa is very small but it gets bigger as you go downstream. The river bed is narrow with a regular slight drop and the rapids are technical.

This section is isolated and access is difficult except at the shrine of Montgarri. Difficult rapids are obvious and can be carried. Look out for trees, especially where it's narrow. This is in a wonderful setting and it makes a **dream run**.

SECTION B (upper)

14 km class IV-V   Kayaking ★★★   Scenery ★★★

Put in

Whether coming from France or Spain, the best access is via the village of **Esterri d'Aneu** where you take the road towards Boren and Alos d'Isil. After 6 km you pass the barrage of Boren. From the village **Alos d'Isil** you take the only road (which becomes a track on leaving the village) for 14.5 km until you reach the third foot bridge which crosses from the left to the right bank. This is the put in.

Take out

At the Boren barrage as noted above.

Description

This section is both big and technical and changes drastically with water level.

At low levels it is continuous class IV that can usually be paddled at sight with only two big class 5 rapids. At high water levels it is seriously continuous class V+ : then the eddies are few, the water is very powerful and the two big rapids may be un-runnable.

The end of the canyon-like stretch can be class 5 and must be taken on the extreme left. This rapid is about 2 km upstream of the village of Alos d'Isil and can be scouted from the road. The second large class 5 rapid can also be seen from the road about 2.5 km upstream from the village of Isil.

Again, like Section A, the setting of this run is magnificent!

SECTION C   (from Escalo to Llavorsi)

8 km of mostly class II   Kayaking ★★   Scenery ★

Put in
At the village of Escalo.

Take out
You can take out about 300 metres upstream of the village of Llavorsi or continue down the next class III stretch which has a weir that can usually be shot in the middle.

Description
This section can be scouted from the road that runs along its length. As you would guess from its grading it is not very difficult, the river flowing quietly between trees.

For those looking for more excitement it is possible to put in above Escalo, by the hydro outlet 800m below the dam. The gradient on this short section is continuous for the first kilometre giving class IV to V rapids depending on the water level, then the gradient eases off and the rapids slow down to class III until you reach Escalo.

SECTION D   ('Classic').

35 km of class III-IV+ D   Kayaking ★★★   Scenery ★★

Put in
At the village of **Llavorsi.**

Take out
At the exit of the **Gorge of Collegats** at the official car park. On the river this is 500m after the second raod tunnel.

Description
You can paddle this river as several runs or do the whole 35 km in one day since it is high volume with a strong current. (This is a deservedly popular section for commercial rafting.)

The part from **Llavorsi to Rialp** is the most continuous with rapids of class IV+. After Rialp and about 3 km above Sort look out for a **dangerous dam** that must be portaged on the left. (Sort is famous for its Slalom site and will be the location for the World Rodeo Championships in 2001)

The 3 km downstream of **Sort** are class II, then the descent becomes wilder again with some class IV rapids at Baro (with names such as 'El Pastis', and La Banana). In the extremely scenic **Gorge of Collegats** there are no difficult rapids but beware of getting pinned on rocks by the current.

Río Caregue (or Berasti)

4 km of class IV+ D   Kayaking ★★   Scenery ★

The River

It is difficult to know the exact name of this river since the rivers Caregue and Berasti flow into each other and the maps give no indication which one is the major one. However this river is a tributary of the right bank of the Noguera Pallaresa, joining it at the village of **Rialp**. The river is fed by run off from the surrounding high peaks but the water catchment is not extensive and so the river is better paddled from the time of thaw to around about the middle of May.

Put in

500 metres after the exit from Rialp going back up the valley take the left road in the direction of the village of Caregue. About 4 km after the turning take the track on the left leading to the confluence of the Caregue or Berasti and the Pomano.

Take out

At **Rialp** at the road bridge of the N 147.

Description

This is a river with a steep gradient, narrow and littered with rocks. There is an artificial **weir** one-third of the way that is completely un-runnable and should be portaged on the right bank. The most sustained section is after this weir. Always beware of trees which may force you to carry.

Río Lladorre

1 km of class III (4)   Kayaking ★★   Scenery ★★★

The River

The river Lladorre has its source in mountain peaks rising to close on 3000 metres and the valley catchment is extensive enough to allow paddling throughout the month of May.

Put in

From the village of Llavorsi take the road to the village of Alins, then turn left towards the village of **Tavascan**. As you leave this village continue straight ahead on the track. The put in is one kilometre above the dam and where a large tributary comes in on the right bank.

Take out

The take out is at the **dam** well upstream of **Tavascan.**

Description

This run is in a superb setting but unfortunately is rather short. When we paddled it there was unluckily no water below the dam so we couldn't paddle this lower section - but it looked interesting.....

Río Noguera de Vallferrera

4 km of class IV-V E   Kayaking ★ ★ ★   Scenery ★ ★ ★

The River
This wild, mountainous run has no water extraction points and it can be paddled throughout the thaw period from May to the beginning of June.

Put in
From the village of Llavorsi take the road to Alins. From there take the main road along the river. After leaving the village of **Areu** the road becomes a car track along which you continue to drive until the first bridge takes you to the left bank. 1.2 km further on the track divides into two. Take the one on the right which winds steeply upwards. The put in is where it meets the Vallferrera.

Take out
1.2 km upstream of the bridge mentioned above, take the left track immediately after the a little bridge on the right. The track straightens out but remains passable and brings you to a water outlet pipe some 100m upstream. This is the take out point.

Description
This river is a real treasure! The paddling is fun and continuous from beginning to end - in a wild setting with alternating technical and bigger stretches. At higher water levels most of the paddling can be done at sight but always beware of trees. At lower water levels most of the rapids become class V and the run becomes very testing.
   We advise you to try to gauge the level of the water at the take out before getting on the river.

Río Noguera de Tor

4.5 km of Class IV+   Kayaking ★ ★   Scenery ★ ★

The River
Although the catchment area is limited, this river is fed from the melting snows of mountains up to 2900m and thus it normally sustains good water levels during May.

Put In
From Llavorsi go to the small village of **Alins** and there take the right turn onto the track heading towards **Tor**. The put in is about 4.5 km upstream of the first bridge below a rocky stretch visible from the track.

Take Out
This is 300m upstream of the bridge mentioned above and just before the start of the gorge stretch.

Description
The gradient of the river is regular but the flow can be swift in high water. The narrow bed of the river makes paddling somewhat technical, challenging, and satisfying. This river compares well with the better known Gave d'Aydius.

Río Santa Magdalena (or Romodriu)

10 km of class IV-V D   Kayaking ★★   Scenery ★★

The River

The Rio Magdalena is a tributary of the Noguero Pallaresa which it joins 3 km downstream of **Llavorsi**.

Snow melt from the surrounding mountains (up to 2800m) which means that this river is at its best during May - but note that due to the hydro-electric extraction the water level is only high enough for paddling **at the peak of the thaw period.**

Put In

Go down the valley from Llavorsi and after crossing the Rio Romadriu take the left track towards the village of **Montenarto**. After 5 km again take a track to the left to the hamlet of **Romadriu** with the river below. The put in is below the water abstraction point.

Take Out

This is at the confluence of the Rio Romadriu and Rio Noguera Pallaresa.

Description

This narrow river is technical throughout the run. To avoid a wasted journey via Montenarto the level of water can assessed from the track leading upstream from the take out at the confluence.

Río Manyanet

4 km of class IV-V-VI (xxx) E   Kayaking ★★   Scenery ★★

The River

This river is the principal tributary of the Rio Flamicell which itself flows into the Rio Noguera Pallaresa near **La Pobla de Segur**. The catchment is limited and only rapid snow melt in **May** supplies sufficient water for paddling.

Put In

On the N260 from Pont de Suert and Senterada take the left turn on the descent of the Col de Perves and go through the villages of **Iglesies** and Xerallo. After the latter the road becomes a track leading up the valley to the hamlet of **Manyanet**. The river below is reached on foot.

Take out

This is down the valley where the road rejoins the river.

Description

When we made our descent we had to make a 800m portage of one steep section, but this might be runnable in lower water. The lines of the rest of the run are fairly obvious although the river is narrow.

The approach to the portage is fore-warned by a succession of small ledges where stopping is difficult and finally a large hole and a further ledge. The difficult portage is made via the right bank.

Río Bellera (or Bugia)

8 km of Class III-IV (5)   Kayaking ★★   Scenery ★

The River
This is the name given to the Rio Manyanet below the village of **Les Iglesies**.

Put In
At the downstream side of the village of **Xerallo.**

Take Out
At the village of **Senterada.**

Description
This is a pleasant but technical river to paddle - watch out for fallen trees. There are roadworks at present in progress which may affect the river.

Vallée du río Manyanet.

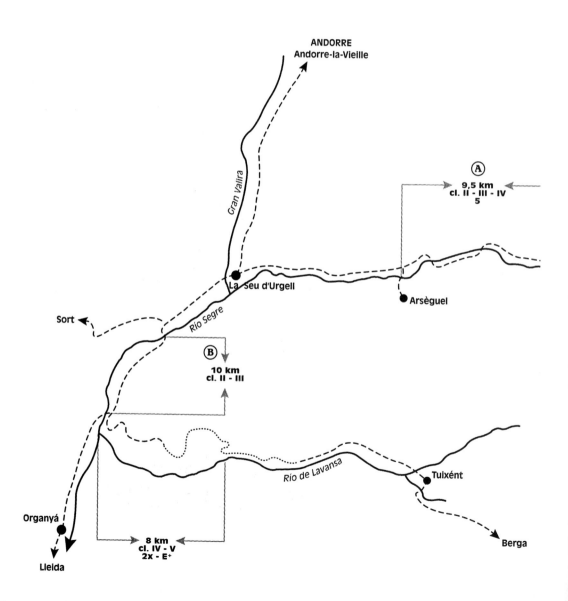

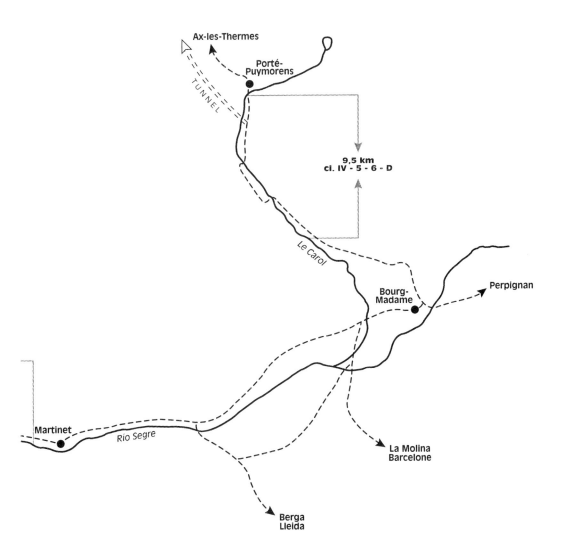

Ax-les-Thermes

Porté-
Puymorens

TUNNEL

9,5 km
cl. IV - 5 - 6 - D

Le Carol

Bourg-
Madame

Perpignan

Martinet

Río Segre

La Molina
Barcelone

Berga
Lleida

BASSIN
DU RÍO SEGRE

BASSIN
DU RÍO SEGRE

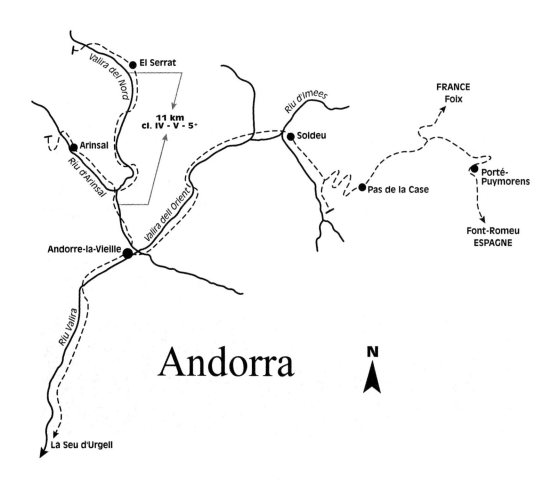

Bassin Río Segre

Tourist Offices

LA SEU D'URGELL (25700)
TORISMO
Pg. Joan Brudieu
Tel : 973 35 09 91

Rafting & Kayak Companies

Parc Olimpic del Segre
25700 La Seu d'Urgell
Tel : 973 36 00 92
Fax : 973 73 36 01 92

Sierra de Cadí.

Río Segre

The River

The Rio Segre is devoid of hydro-electric installations on the sections described and is navigable from mid April to mid June.

SECTION A

9.5 km of class II-III-IV (5)   Kayaking ★   Scenery ★

Put In

At 1.5 km above the village of **Martinet** where the whole of the flow above is returned.

Take Out

About 9.5 km down the valley from the put in, turn off towards the village of **Arseguel** and after 200m leave the vehicles at a road bridge.

Description

This is a river with a large bed and many Class II-III sections. The biggest problems are between two road bridges where a part of the river is canalised on the left bank. Some passages are visible from the road including a 2 m dam which is by passed on the right of a large upright rock.

SECTION B

10 km of Class II-III   Kayaking ★★   Scenery ★

Put In

Under the N 260 road bridge downstream of the village of **Adrall**.

Take Out

At the next bridge downstream at the start of the **Gorges de Tresponts**.

Description

Good waves mark this section but only in high water. A dam at the half way point can be shot, but not at high water levels because of a stopper.

Le Carol

9.5 km of class IV (5) (6) D   Kayaking ★★   Scenery ★★

The River

This river has the distinction that you can put on in France and then paddle into Spain. The river then joins the Rio Segre high up near **Bourg Madame**.

This torrent is fed from late April to the end of May thaws and during heavy rain or any early warm periods at the end of winter.

Put In

At the road bridge on the N 20 downstream of the village of **Porte-Puymorens**.

Take Out

At the large parking area 2 km upstream of the village of **Latour de Carol** on the N 20. Do not confuse the latter with the ruins of Tour Carol about 5 km upstream and again on the N 20.

Description

The 'Defile de la Faou' immediately after the put in, sets the mood for the descent. According to water level the ledge here can have a stopper and also there may be danger from fallen trees within the narrow passage of the defile. This section can be examined from the road.

After the defile a large amount of water enters from a conduit at the right bank. 3 km further down the first barrage can be portaged on the right, or by a rather derelict slide, to lead to the first Class 5 stretch of drops of 5 and then 8 m.

When the road crosses to the opposite bank a second barrage must be portaged. A second Class 5+ drop should be examined before attempting - it consists of a ledge and an impressive drop.
Below here is a Class 6 drop which can be scouted on the way up the road - it is located about 1.5 km above the take out.

A gauge indicating the **water level** is found under the first bridge upstream of Latour Carol. 115 on the scale is medium water. At levels below this the section between the barrages may not be passable.

Río de Lavansa

8 km of class IV-V (xx) E+   Kayaking ★   Scenery ★★★

The River

This right bank tributary of the Rio Segre drains the Sierra de Cadi a little to the south of the Pyrenees proper. The summits of 2000-2500 m mean it is well supplied with water during the rapid thaws in May or in a warm spell during April. There are no hydro-electric installations.

Put In

Take the N 1313 south from La Seu d'Urgell and after about 30 km take the left fork before a bridge to head towards **Montan** and **Tuixen**. Put in where the road rejoins the river after about 10 km.

Take Out

Continue a short distance down the N 1313 from the turn off to the put in and leave the vehicles level with the confluence of the Rio Segre about 300 m below this fork..

Description

The classification of this section does not take into account the stress of a passage through such an incredibly deep, narrow, and committing canyon which is **comparable to the Grand Canyon du Verdon** (in the French Alps) and this tempted us to place this river under the heading 'For the Record'!

Opportunities for climbing out of the canyon are rare and certainly difficult with a long haul up to the road about 600 m above. A solid team is needed and a flow, we would estimate, of about 3 cumecs.

The first rocky section must be portaged on the left before a tricky crossing of the river via some fallen trunks of trees (if these are still there). From then on the river is quite sporty with good rapids all in a grand setting. Further on you have no choice but to take out in an eddy to the right as the river surges into a hole under two huge vertical rocks which we named 'Le Metro'. You have to portage by climbing over these rocks and then it is tricky to launch again below.

This is a long and arduous trip - very long! Good luck!

Río Valira del Nord

11 km of Class IV-V (5+)   Kayaking ★★   Scenery ★

The River

The Valira del Nord is the main tributary of the Valira d'Orient which drains the whole of Andorra. Summits up to 2800 m feed the river during the May thaw.

Put In

At **Andorre la Vieille** take the road passing through **La Massana** to the village of Ordino. Proceed to **El Serrat** and access the river here at the confluence of the two rivers.

Take Out

This is below the road bridge before the final gorge, just downstream of **La Massana** on the road to the village of Anyos.

Description

This is narrow river with technical passages. The main difficulties are in the upper section with one constriction after a bend to the left and two big drops which join to form a premier piece of action.

After this the run then gets easier as you travel down the river. Make sure that you do not miss the take out as you do not want to attempt the gorge below!

Books and Maps

A selection of other guidebooks and maps to the Pyrenees:

Guidebooks

The Rough Guide - the Pyrenees, by Marc Dubin. 1998. Price £10.99.
An excellent outdoor-orientated guidebook that complements this one. Highly recommended.

Landscapes of the Pyrenees, by Sunflower Books, London. 1998. Around £8.
Small handy full colour guide that highlights the most interesting areas of country and mountain. Good detailed colour maps of short walks and also car tours.

Guide-Itineraires 700 Rivieres de France. Daniel Bonnigal.   Editions la pirogue. 1991. 138 francs.
An impressively detailed guidebook (in French) to almost all the navigable rivers of France.   A good reference source for those "what's that river like that we've just driven by?" enquiries.   However no maps and no illustrations give this a 5 mogadon rating for bedtime reading.

Kayak en Galicia by Andres Sio Gonzalez 1996. Price 135 ff.
A brilliant little guidebook to this beautiful area of NW Spain and Portugal (in French and Spanish).

Maps

Euro Cart. Costa Brava & Pyrenees. 1: 300,000. Price £5
A good clear overall map of the Pyrenees. That covers all of the Pyrenees, both French and Spanish and includes much of NE Spain from Barcelona to Bilbao. Available from specialist travel book stores such as Stanfords in London.

Michelin yellow series. 1:200,000.
These maps are widely available. **Sheets 85 and 86** cover all of the French Pyrenees and most of the Spanish side in reasonable detail. If you are touring through France, then the **Michelin Motoring Atlas of France** at the same scale represents great value for money at around £10.

Canoe-Kayak Map of France. FFCK and IGN. 1993. Price £5. Or 30 francs in France.
Excellent map that shows some 490 rivers, colour coded to show their difficulty; information is given in English, French and German; overprinted on a high quality and detailed road map of France at a scale of 1:1,000,000 - this saves you buying a road map!

Topographic Maps
The French IGN 1:25,000 blue series are excellent and widely available in France, but are probably only of interest if you are spending a lot of time in one area.   Some of these sheets cover the Spanish side of the border, but otherwise good topographic maps of Spain are hard to come by.

Notes
A lot of useful booklets and maps are available (usually free) from local tourist offices)
    Prices are approximate and are for guidance only. The kayaking guidebooks are available either from your local specialist retailer or from 'Le Canotier' - see the Suppliers Directory.

Notes on Contributors

Patrick Santal works in the week as a fireman in the city of Pau but spends his weekends paddling the rivers of the Pyrenees. He is an enthusiastic kayaker who had paddled for many years and he has also worked in the field of outdoor activities including canoeing, caving and canyoning. Experience in other areas like the Alps and Corsica reinforced his belief that the Pyrenees has paddling treasures just as good if not better than these more famous regions. This firm belief encouraged him and fellow club members to research and produce this book.

Alan Fox was founding Chairman of the D.K.C. (Deviants Kayak Club). A man of many talents, cartoonist, film maker, engineer, author, expedition organiser and lecturer. You'll meet him on a world river - or in some low bar. Alan has several books to his credit: his latest cartoon book is 'The Blind Probe'.

Peter Knowles took four years and some epic swims to learn to roll, just in time for a trip down the Grand Canyon in 1973. He was run over by a 35ft motorised raft in one of the rapids, but survived, fell in love with big-water rivers and has had a love-hate relationship with rafts ever since.

In the last twenty years he has run 'quite a lot of rivers' in many different countries and continents, including more than a few first descents. Since 1983 he has mainly been exploring and running the rivers of the Himalaya and was recently selected as one of 20 'modern explorers' in an exhibition at Britain's Royal Geographical Society. More recent adventures include first descents, and filming for American television in Mexico and Bhutan. He now tries to stay warm and dry sitting in front of a word processor, writing about rivers - but friends keep dragging him off to some exotic river to get cold, wet and scared yet again!

Ben Love organised a youth expedition to the Grand Canyon when he was 16 and then seems to have caught that paddlers affliction of never quite finishing his studies and spend the subsequent summer vacations working as a raft guide!) After a couple of seasons in Iceland he decided it was time to seek out warmer climes and as his studies only allowed him to work the northern hemisphere season so Spain beckoned and he has worked in Cantabria and the Pyrenees'.

Phil Quill has been paddling for more years now than he care's to admit although he would like everyone to know that he started very young. He works at the Woodmill Outdoor Centre in Southampton and has been running white water and sea kayaking trips to Spain since 1989 most notably in the Picos de Europa, Galicia, Cataluna and Menorca. His trips are particularly renowned for their evening activities which usually consist of tracking down another great restaurant.

Norman, Pamela and David Taylor were founder members, 14 years ago, of Leeds-based White Rose Canoe Club, Yorkshire's largest and some would say finest. Norman has been BCU Regional Chairman and Access Officer and now heads the Washburn Committee. Paddling expertise in the family is inversely proportional to age - Dave being a veteran of white water and keen polo player with current division winners White Rose polo team and his parents occasionally to be seen shouting at each other in a canoe.

Previous publishing attempts include several BCU Regional Yearbooks and David's 'Yorkshire Rivers - a Canoeists Guide', jointly with Mike Twiggs. A maison secondaire (ex ruin!) on the River Lot in the Midi Pyrenees provides yet another garden full of assorted canoes and an insight into the local French canoeing scene - frenzied groups of children and bewildered tourists with no helmets arriving at the take out over the river.

Glossary

ENGLISH	FRENCH	SPANISH
Bank (river)	Rive	Orilla
Bouyancy	Flottabilite	para flotar
Buoyancy aid	Gilet (de securité)	Chalico salvadidas
Buoyancy bag	Gonfle	
Breakout	Stop	Parada
Bridge	Pont	Puente
Capsize	Chavirer	
Capsize & swim	Désaler	
Class of difficulty	Classe	Grado
Cliff	Falaise	Acantilado
Confluence	Confluence	Confluencia
Current	Courant	Corrinente
Dam	Dam	Embalse
Downstream	En aval	Abajo
Drop (1-2m)	Seuil	
Drop (3m+)	Chute	Salto
Eddy	Contre	Remolino
Eddy-line	Port-feuille	
Eskimo Roll	Esquimoter	
Ferry or shuttle	Navette	
First aid	Premiers secour	Primura ayuda
Flow	Débit	Curso
Follow	Suivre	Seguir
Footbridge	Passerelle	Pasarela
Gauge	Échelle	Nivel
Gorge	Gorge	Garganta
Gorge-like	Engorge	Encajado
Gradient	Dénivelée	Pendiente
Hole	Trou	Rebufo
Left	Gauche	Izquierda
Low	Basse	Bajo
Narrow	Etroit	Estrecho
Navigable	Navigable	Navegable

Glossary

ENGLISH	FRENCH	SPANISH
Paddle (noun)	Pagaie	Canalete
Path	Chemin, sentier.	Pista de tierra
Play-hole	Trou à chandelles	
Pop-out	Chandelle	
Portage	Portage	Porteo
Put-in	Point d'embarquement	Embarco
Rain	Pluie	Lluvia
Rapid	Rapide	Rapido
Ravine	Ravin, canyon	Barranco
Reverse	Marche arrière	Contrario
Right	Droite	Derecha
River	Rivière	Río
River Basin	Bassin	Cuenca
Road	Route	Carretera
Rock	Rocher	Bloque
Rock or boulder	Caillou	Pena
Rolling wave / small stopper	Rouleau*	
Section (of river) or gap	Passage	Paso
Spraydeck	Jupe or Jupette	
Stopper	Rappel	Rebufo
Syphon	Syphon	Sifón
Take-out	Point de débarquement	Llegada / Desembarco
Throw line	Corde de securité	
To paddle	Naviguer	
Tow back	Rappel	Rebufo
Tributary	Affluent	Afluente
Undercut	Drossage	
Un-runnable	Infran (chissable)	Infranqueable
Upstream	En amont	Arriba
Water level	Niveau	Nivel
Waterfall)	Cascade	Cascada
Wave	Vague	Ola
Weir	Barrage	Embalse

Adour   73
Adour Bassin 71
Adour de Lesponne   73
Ainsa   130
Alet   94
Alet upper 95
Alins   165
Andorra   174
Anso   120
Aoiz   116
Ara   131
Ara Bassin 129
Arac   93
Aragón   123
Aragon Bassin 110
Aragón Subordán   121
Arce   114
Areu   165
Argeles-Gazost   61, 62
Ariege   100
Ariege Bassin   97
Arive   115
Arreau   77, 79
Arrens   61
Arrieta   114
Arroya   26
Artozqui   115
Asasp   49
Aso   142
Aspe   49
Aston   102
Aude   106
Aulus les Bains   93
Aure   77
Auzat   101
Ax les Thermes   100
Axat   106, 107
Aydius   51
Ayerbe   126, 127
Azun   62

Bagneres de Bigorre   73
Baliera   155
Barbaruens   149
Barranco de Llert   149
Barranco de Viú   148
Barrosa   143
Barruara   156
Bastan   37, 65

Baudean   73
Bedous   49
Bellera   167
Benasque   147, 148
Berasti   164
Bergua   133
Biddarray   35, 37
Bielsa   138, 143
Biert   93
Biescas   126
Boltana   133
Bonansa   151
Books   175
Boren   162
Bossost   85
Bourg Madame   173
Broto   132
Brousset   53
Bugia   167
Bujaruelo   131
Burgui   119
Buzy   56

Cares   25
Class of difficulty   15
Contributors   176
Conversions   15
Countries   22
Cumecs   15

Deva   25
Difficulty classification   15
Driving   21

Ebro   26
Erce   93
Eriste   148
Esca   119
Escalo   163
Esera   147
Esera Bassin 145
Esterri d'Aneu   162
Estos   148
Estours   92

Fauna 28
Ferrieres   61
Fiscal   132, 133
Fish   28

Flore   28
Flying   19
Fonchanina   155
Forcos   133
Fort du Portalet   49
France   22

Gabas   53, 55
Gallego   126
Gallego Bassin   124
Garbet   93
Garonne Bassin 82
Gavarnie   68
Gave d'Azun   62
Gave d'Oloron   48
Gave d'Arrens   61
Gave d'Aspe   49
Gave d'Aydius   51
Gave de Cauterets   63
Gave de Gavarnie   68
Gave de Larrau   42
Gave de Pau   60
Gave de Ste. Engrace   43
Gave d'Heas   67
Gave d'Ossau   55
Gave du Bastan   65
Gave du Brousset   53
Gave du Lourdios   51
Gave du Saison   41
Gedre   67, 68
Ger   84
Gesse   106
Glossary   178
Grade of difficulty   15
Grande Nive   35

Heas   67
Hecho   121
Hydrology   29
Hydro-speeding   31

Igliesies   166, 167
Insurance   19
International grading   15
Iraty   115
Irues   143
Isabeña   151
Itoiz   114
Itxassou   36

Kayaking Pyrenees 17
Kercabanac 91, 93

Lafortunada 138, 143
Larrau 41, 42
Laruns 56
Laspuna 143
Lavansa 173
Lesponne 73
Lez 90
Lladorre 164
Llavorsi 163
Llert 149
Loudenvielle 78
Lourdes 60
Lourdios 51
Louron 78
Lumbier 116, 118
Luz-Saint-Sauveur 65

Mallos de Rigos 126
Manyanet 166
Maps 175
Marsa 107
Martinet 172
Massana 174
Mauleon Barousse 84
Mauleon Licharre 40
Mediterraneen Bassin 103
Miegebat 55
Murillo de Gallego 127

Nantilla 106
Neste d'Aure 77
Neste de Louron 78
Nestes Bassin 75
Nive Bassin 33
Nive des Aldudes 38
Nive d'Esterençuby 38
Noguera de Tor (Pallaresa) 165
Noguera de Tor (Ribagorçana) 156
Noguera de Vallferrera 165
Noguera Pallaresa 162
Noguera Pallaresa Bassin 157
Noguera Ribagorçana Bassin 152
North Coast of Spain 25

Oloron 48
Oloron Bassin 45

Oriege 100
Orlu 100
Ossau 55
Osses 35, 38
Ourse 84
Oust 93
Ouzom 61

Pamplona 110
Pau 60
Pau Bassin 57
Permits 18, 25
Picos de Europa 25
Pierrefitte Nestalas 60, 64
Planning 19
Pobla de Segur 166
Pollution 28
Pont de la Taule 91, 94
Pont de'Suert 152, 156
Prat 78
Puenta la Reina 121
Pyrenees 17
Quillan 103

Rafting 31
Rainfall 29
Rebenty 107
Rialp 163, 164
Ribeira 155
Riberot 90
Rioumajou 80
Rodes 108
Romodriu 166

Sabinanigo 124
Saison Bassín 39
Salat 90
Salat Bassin 87
Salau 90, 91
Salazar 118
Salvatierra 119
San Juan de Plan 139, 140
Sanguesa 116
Santa Magdalena 166
Security 19
Segre 172
Segre Bassin 168
Seira 149
Sella 25

Serraduy 151
Seu d'Urgell 171
Sia 69, 127
Snowfall 30
Snowmelt 29
Soeix 50
Sort 163
Soueix 91
Spain 18, 23, 25.
St Girons 90
St Lary 77, 80
St. Jean-Pied-de-Port 35, 38
St. Lizier d'Ustou 94
Ste. Engrace 43
Stillom 94, 95
Storms 29
Summary of rivers 8
Surfing 22, 26

Tamezaigues 80
Tarascon 101
Tardets 40
Tavascan 164
Tech 109
Tet 108
Thaw 30
Tor 165
Torla 131, 132
Tuixen 173

Uhaitxa 43
Urrizate 37
Urrobi 114
Urtxuria 117
Using this guide 15
Usun 118

Valira Del Nord 174
Vallferrera 165
Vallibierna 147
Varrados 85
Vellos 142
Veral 120

Water levels 15
When to paddle 15, 29

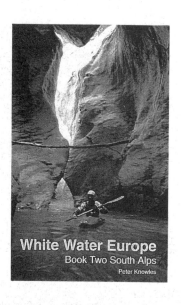

ECOLE DE **P**AGAIE

LOCATION DE **B**ATEAUX

SCHWETZINGEN - ALLEMAGNE